RIDING A DRESSAGE TEST

Riding a Dressage Test

Martin Diggle
and
Terry Colgate

J.A. Allen
London

British Library Cataloguing in Publication Data
A catalogue record for this book is available from the British Library

ISBN 0-85131-615-8

First published 1989
Second edition 1994

Published in Great Britain by
J. A. Allen & Company Limited
1 Lower Grosvenor Place, Buckingham Palace Road,
London SW1W OEL

Typeset by Textype Typesetters, Cambridge
Printed and bound in Hong Kong by Dah Hua Printing Press Co. Ltd.

Acknowledgements

The authors wish to thank the following people for their contributions to this book:
Bob Love B.H.S.A.I. and Marian Pattison B.H.S.I.I. for informative conversations concerning the judge's viewpoint. John Cherrington R.I.B.A. for his ability to draw dressage figures better than he rides them.

Contents

— Contents —

List of Illustrations

Preface

Many riders, especially those who are not horse owners or convinced dressage enthusiasts, do not enter their first test because of a conviction that they have elevated equitation to an art form; they do so because someone badgers them into 'having a go', or because it is an unavoidable precursor to the 'exciting' phases of a horse trial.

Having succumbed to coercion, or bowed to the inevitable, the rider is confronted with a test sheet which seems to consist of impossibly complicated or hopelessly inadequate instructions. Attempts to commit the test to memory result in midnight incantations, ritual dances in the garden, and increasingly worried neighbours.

Eventually, the day dawns when the competitor must try to translate the cause of his insomnia into a display of equine grace – possibly on an unfamiliar horse who looks, and moves, as though there is a prepotent element of dinosaur in his pedigree. Two minutes before the start of the test, total amnesia replaces the black despair of the practise arena, and the rider drifts through the movements like a sleepwalker in a maze, to be damned with faint praise by a judge who is desperate for a cup of coffee.

Strangely, this fairly standard introduction to riding a dressage test does not put many people off. For the most part, they reappear at the next competition with an air of martyrdom and a flask of strong drink. This must, presumably, be because they feel there is something to be gained from the experience – and some people confess to enjoying it!

This book is written in the hope that it will persuade more riders teetering on the brink to brave the test arena, by explaining the purposes, aims and principles of dressage, and how to go about riding a test whilst minimising the traumas outlined above.

Introduction

The term 'dressage' has, historically, evoked mixed reactions from riders, especially in Britain. For many years it was considered almost synonymous with 'circus tricks', and it is somewhat ironic that the Englishman James Fillis – later to be widely acknowledged as a great trainer – did much of his early work in the (French) circus, this being initially the only place where his skills were appreciated.

While general opinion had undoubtedly changed since those days, many people still have somewhat extreme ideas and attitudes concerning dressage. For some, it is nothing more than riders in funny hats gyrating *ad nauseum* in a confined space, while others will see displays by the Spanish Riding School or Cadre Noir, and think of dressage solely in terms of equestrian ballet; beautiful, but entirely beyond the reach of 'ordinary' riders. At a more mundane level, dressage is often considered the province of those who dislike jumping, or perceived as an activity entirely divorced from 'normal' riding.

Although these images (except the last) may all contain an element of truth, they are only tiny and highly coloured fragments of the whole picture. Dressage is, in fact, the broadest of the equestrian disciplines and has a fundamental influence upon all the others. The word means, quite simply, 'training' and this is something which all ridden horses must undergo, and continue to undergo (for better or worse) each time they are ridden.

The extent and type of training will depend (among other things) upon the use to which the horse is being put, but *all* horses will be better prepared for work in their chosen sphere if they move freely and correctly, and are well-balanced and obedient.

Of course, equating dressage to training does not produce an inevitable link between schooling and riding tests, and those whose riding revolves around various school horses may argue that they do not ride any horse with sufficient regularity to have an overall impact upon his training, so how can there be any justification for their participating in 'training' competitions. On a wider basis, the question may be asked as to why anyone – owner or hirer – should bother to ride dressage tests unless they are either committed enthusiasts, or horse trials competitors who have the dressage phase thrust upon them.

There are several answers to this question, and the degree of relevance of each will depend upon the circumstances of the individual.

Firstly, a simple dressage test performed in an enclosed arena affords an ideal introduction to competitive riding for the keen novice. Apart from the fact that such a rider may not yet be sufficiently experienced to participate in any form of jumping competition, the relatively calm atmosphere of one horse in a confined area is inherently safer than a probably more excited horse in a large field with a number of others. However, while riding a dressage test should be a safe affair, it will provide an introduction to performing under a measure of stress (remembering the test, riding in isolation from an instructor, riding to the best of one's ability and trying to 'get it right first time') and this is experience which will be of value and relevance to all forms of competitive riding.

Secondly, it should be appreciated that, except at the upper levels or in major competitions, dressage tests can generally be considered less as a competition against other horses and riders, and more as a competition against individual circumstances. It is not so much a case of 'can I beat so and so?' as of 'can we do better than last time?' or 'how well can I get this horse to perform?'. Thus (although it is certainly pleasant to win), the key issue may be not so much the actual placing but rather the assessment of progress, either of an established horse/rider partnership or of the rider's ability to produce a good performance from any given horse.

Of course, it can be argued that a rider's (or horse's) progress can be assessed by their regular instructor, and this is certainly true. However, there may well be advantages in having an occasional assessment by an experienced judge who is taking a fresh, impartial view in a more formal setting. This is not to imply that judges are necessarily more knowledgeable than instructors (many people perform both roles), it is simply a question of circumstance. The instructor who teaches a pupil on a regular basis is almost inevitably going to compare what he sees with previous lessons; the horse/rider will be perceived as going either better or worse than last time. Also, there will be an understandable tendency to give 'second chances' and evaluate on the basis of best results ('try it again, only this time do so and so . . . that's much better'). This is, of course, part of the instructor's brief, but it does not give a totally accurate assessment of what horse and rider can achieve in isolation – which is the true test of progress. Furthermore, it must be admitted that it is in an instructor's interest to emphasise areas of improvement, since this is what the pupil is paying for. (Instructors who feel that this comment is a slur upon their integrity should consider how often they tell pupils – other than the most highly-motivated and self-critical – that a performance is insufficient, let alone bad or very bad. They should also ask themselves how many clients they would retain if they were to be that frank.)

These considerations and influences should not affect the dressage judge. He will, ideally, be unfamiliar with the competitors and should, in any case, assess only what he sees during the course of the test. These factors will help him to judge the performance in absolute terms, that is, to assess movements strictly in accordance with the principles of equitation rather than by reference to the partnership's 'norm'.

For the owner-rider, or anyone who has a regular partnership with a horse, the value of such an assessment is self-evident, even if not guaranteed to boost the ego. However, the experience of preparing for and riding a dressage test can, in some respects, be of equal (or even greater) value to the non-owner. Assessing a horse during a fairly short 'riding-in' time, and then trying to produce the best one-off performance possible is certainly no easy task, but for anyone who is really trying it is a thought-provoking business, and will help to produce a thinking, open-minded rider. Furthermore, the diversity of horses likely to be encountered should add to the rider's repertoire, and enlarge his 'vocabulary' of communication to a greater extent than might be the case if he always rode the same horse.

As an illustration of the possibilities, the occasion is recalled when, at a judges course, two proficient club riders each rode a 'guinea-pig' test on their own horses, and then swopped mounts and re-rode the tests. Both horses were universally judged to have performed better for the non-owners. While it cannot be assumed that such a result would be typical of this equine version of 'musical chairs', it certainly provides food for thought.

Reverting to consideration of dressage as a phase of horse trials, it is undoubtedly true that there are some riders who think of it as a preliminary penance, which has to be endured before proceeding to the exciting phases. However, it must be assumed that this penance affords them some degree of masochistic pleasure, or else they would confine their activities to other forms of competition. Of course, some horses and riders are, by nature, more suited to the challenge of cross-country than to the confines of the dressage arena, but it is obviously in the interests of any horse trials competitor to try and do as well as possible in the dressage phase. Not only will enhanced performance here improve their chances in the overall competition, but more attention to correct training 'on the flat' will, as we have seen, assist in making the horse a better ride all round.

In this context, it is interesting to note that there are still some people who feel that 'doing dressage' will prove detrimental to the horse's performance in showjumping or cross-country. However, provided that the dressage consists of correct training and not 'upsetting the horse in a confined space', this attitude is without foundation, as a study of top-level Horse Trials results will prove. It may, incidentally, be useful for the Horse Trials rider to make the occasional visit to a dressage-only competition, with a view to gaining a little extra practice and experience, and perhaps freshen the performance of horse and rider by riding a less familiar test.

Whilst it is hoped that these reasons for riding dressage tests will be appreciated, it must be admitted that the emphasis has, so far, been upon the logic of doing so, rather than upon any inherent pleasure. Since it is not the purpose of this book to persuade the reader to perform tests merely because 'they are good for you', let us look a little more at the aspects of enjoyment and satisfaction involved.

Obviously, the amount of enjoyment and satisfaction derived from any activity is closely linked to one's interest in it and, for many people, interest in dressage is likely to increase with riding experience. Indeed, at an early stage, many riders will give dressage no consideration at all. In common with keen beginners in other fields, they will be partly absorbed by the basics and partly impatient to 'have a go' at those aspects of their new interest which seem most thrilling, and the fact is that few will perceive dressage as fitting into either category. Such attitudes will often persist until the rider has reached the stage at which he is able to obtain walk, trot and canter more or less to command, at which time he may go through a short period of feeling that he has 'arrived'.

However, just as a budding musician will soon realise that there is more to his art than thumping out a three-chord semblance of his favourite tune, so the keen rider will soon start to re-evaluate his own abilities. In the light of increasing personal experience and more informed observation, he will begin to desire greater precision and effectiveness in his riding, and to enquire about correct training techniques, as opposed to expedients which may produce a superficial response. As he places greater emphasis upon refining his techniques and improving communication with the horse, the rider will become increasingly aware of the pleasure of having a large, powerful animal respond willingly and correctly to his aids. Once a rider has experienced – however fleetingly – the sensation of riding a horse who is really 'on the aids' (active, balanced, attentive and obedient), he will never be truly satisfied with any lesser response. It is the search for this sensation which is the fundamental purpose of dressage, and it is by performing tests that one's progress can be readily demonstrated and evaluated. At a more exalted level, the demonstration may blossom into a celebration of harmony between horse and rider and, even i most of us do not aspire to such heights, the moments when it 'all comes right' are still distinctly memorable.

Finally, we can confirm the attraction of competitive dressage by reference to the status of riders drawn from other disciplines. Famous and obvious examples include former World Champion Reiner Klimke and two of Britain's most successful exponents, Jennie Loriston-Clarke and Chris Bartle. Dr. Klimke was European Horse Trials Champion in 1959, Jennie Loriston-Clarke has ridden at top level in numerous equestrian sports, and Chris Bartle was formerly a successful point-to-point and horse trials enthusiast. Riders of such stature, experience and courage would hardly have taken a major interest in dressage unless they had found it to be challenging and stimulating – and their experience in other fields had confirmed the necessity of correct training.

1

Preliminary Considerations

The Rider

Obviously, in order to attempt dressage tests, a rider must have already attained some degree of ability – the question under consideration being, how much?.

The answer to this question is somewhat ambivalent. Since dressage means training, no-one can truly be said to be 'riding dressage' until such time as their overall effect is to improve the horse's way of going. However, in practice, a rider may well be capable of producing the movements of a basic (preliminary level) test before he has reached such a standard. This, of course, highlights the fact that persuading a horse to perform a move-ment does not necessarily equate to persuading him to perform it correctly or well (a point which all riders should bear in mind).

Nonetheless, given the capability to produce the broad require-ments of the test, the keen, enquiring rider should find the experience valuable, and there should be a consequent long-term benefit to the horse(s) he rides. In this respect, dressage differs from activities involving jumping, in which an imbalance of ambition over ability creates a high risk of injury and detriment to both horse and rider. Provided that the rider is neither mounted on a palpably unsuitable horse, nor attempting to train the horse unsupervised, problems of this magnitude should not occur in dressage.

Thus a rider can gainfully start to perform preliminary level tests once he can obtain and maintain walk, trot and canter, and ride basic school figures on his proposed mount. These are obviously the minimum requirements, since, until this level is reached, the rider will be unable to conform to the requirements of any test. For the purposes of this book, therefore, it is assumed

15

that the reader has attained such a standard of riding, and has a knowledge of the basic principles commensurate with his practical ability. (The basics of riding are dealt with in another book in this series – *Riding From Scratch*).

The Horse

We have already established that this book is not necessarily addressed to owner-riders, and those who are not owners may have little, if any, choice of the horses they ride. Furthermore, we are assuming that many readers who *are* owners will have acquired their horse on the basis of his being generally acceptable and affordable, and that the acquisition may well have been made without competition dressage being the primary target. In 'considering the horse' it is not, therefore, our intention to be concerned with those aspects of temperament and physique which would characterise the ultimate 'dressage horse'. However, since he is an essential element of the business, and it is largely *his* performance which is being assessed, it is worthwhile considering the minimum practical requirements of the horse, as of the rider.

The first requirements are that the horse should be at least moderately fit, in good health, and sound. These factors apply, of course, to any horse who is to be ridden at all, and it may be thought that they are too obvious to be worthy of mention. However, observation suggests that they are sometimes overlooked, and not only at a basic level. Furthermore, in practice, these matters are often not completely cut and dry; while, for instance, a horse may be correctly considered unfit to compete in a hunter trial, it may be thought that performing a dressage test 'won't do him any harm'. This may be true in many cases, but the fact remains that, if a physical problem exists, it will inevitably manifest itself sufficiently to impair the horse's performance. This is especially the case where there is a problem with soundness; not only will any competent judge eliminate a horse who is obviously lame, he will also note any slight unlevelness, and its detrimental effect upon the rhythm and regularity of the gaits, and this will be reflected in his marking.

Purity of movement is, however, not only impaired by actual unsoundness, but also by problems such as dishing, plaiting, brushing and forging. These may result entirely from faults of conformation, but they may also be caused, or accentuated by, deficiencies in fitness and training. Where conformation is the main factor, the rider will have to accept that the horse will never be marked as well as if he were free from the defect concerned.

Expanding upon the topic of conformation, it must be accepted that any fault will, to some degree, detract from the horse's ability to move in ideal fashion – which is why the fault is considered as such. However, since the vast majority of horses fall short of perfection, the rider must seek to minimise the effects of the imperfections by correct riding. Obviously, however well a horse is ridden, his skeletal structure will not be enhanced (although *bad* riding can certainly have a detrimental effect), but there are ways in which good riding can materially lessen the effects of indifferent conformation. Firstly, in some areas defects may not be wholly skeletal (for example neck, quarters) and correct remedial riding will improve the relevant musculature and reduce or remove the fault. Secondly, one aspect of good riding is that it tends to engender greater willingness in the horse. This, of itself, does not have a primary impact upon faults of conformation – indeed 'good riding' may sometimes be made manifest by the rider recognising physical flaws and being prepared to 'work with what he's got'. However, whether the rider's actions alleviate specific difficulty/discomfort in the horse, or whether they just generally encourage him to enjoy his job, there is no doubt that the more willing the horse is, the more likely he is to exhibit the fundamental characteristics (free forward movement and impulsion) of correct movement, and the overall effect will be to minimise the impact of any physical shortcomings.

It is, therefore, in the rider's interest to develop an appreciation of the main points of conformation, in order that he can assess possible problems and be prepared to ride accordingly. Also, of course, such knowledge will be invaluable in the event of acquiring a horse, since it should ensure that animals of congenitally and irrevocably bad conformation are avoided.

The final basic requirement of the horse is that he should be sufficiently well-trained to be able to perform the test concerned. This applies to any level of dressage, but, just as the minimum requirement of the rider is that he can apply the aids for basic movements in walk, trot and canter, so the minimum requirement of the horse is that he recognise, and respond to, these aids. A horse who is too inexperienced, insufficiently or incorrectly trained, or spoilt by constant bad riding, will not be capable of performing any test to a worthwhile standard, and attempting to ride a test on such a horse will merely result in mutual frustration. While the horse owner will have control over these criteria, it is by no means unknown for the rider who hires a horse to have thrust upon him an animal who barely meets them, or even falls short in some respect. This situation reflects little credit upon the establishment responsible but (providing the horse is not actually sick or lame) the rider may – especially if a member of a club team – have little option but to try his best. How he should proceed in such circumstances will be discussed in due course.

2

The Objects and Principles
of Dressage

If a dressage test is to be viewed as a demonstration of a horse's training – and that is certainly how the judge will view it – then it is important for the rider to be aware of the basic objects and principles of correct training. Should he have the good fortune to be riding an already well-trained horse, he can use such knowledge to show off that training to best advantage; should he be less fortunate in his mount, he can apply it in order to produce whatever improvement he can during his time in the saddle.

These basic objects and principles hold good at all levels, and must be given consideration whether the rider is a club member on a hired horse, or a competitor at the Olympics, This is not, of course, to say that they can always be pursued or applied with equal facility; the practical constraints of the horse's physique, temperament and prior training, and the rider's own level of ability are all major influences here. However, it is only by giving credence to these objects and principles that anything resembling correct riding/training will occur.

Let us, therefore, consider precisely what dressage is seeking to achieve, and examine the main factors which indicate the level of achievement reached.

Basic Objectives

The basic objectives of dressage are to improve the horse's standard of training on both a physical and mental level:

Physically the aim is to produce a fit, supple, light in hand, well-balanced athlete who is able to carry himself and his rider to optimum effect.

Mentally the aim is to produce a calm, happy horse, who

19

understands and accepts the rider's aids, and carries out his wishes with willing obedience.

These objects should be pursued and developed in harmony, since there are important links and interactions between them. If it is physically difficult for a horse to carry out his rider's wishes, this will be reflected in his mental attitude; he may become confused, worried, upset or obstinate. If it is mentally difficult for him to do so (that is, if he does not understand what is required, or does not want – for whatever reason – to obey), then he is unlikely to perform the exercise properly, and thus the physical effect/benefit sought will be reduced, negated or counteracted.

Characteristics of Correct Training

Since these are manifestations of the basic objectives, it is not surprising that they, too, are interlinked – in fact to the extent of being largely interdependent. However, it is worthwhile discussing them individually, since they encapsulate the criteria by which dressage tests are assessed.

QUALITY OF GAITS The basic gaits (walk, trot, canter and transverse gallop) are the horse's natural modes of progression but, while most horses can move in these gaits, it does not necessarily follow that they will do so well. There are various factors which influence gait quality, the main ones being health, fitness, soundness, conformation, shoeing and skill of rider. As far as training is concerned, the obvious objective is to manipulate these factors in a manner which enhances the quality of the gaits, or, where a horse exhibits good natural gaits, to avoid doing anything which spoils them. The criteria by which gait quality is assessed are freedom and regularity, which, taken together, will make for purity of gait.

Freedom implies an absence of tension or restraint, whether originating from mental resistance in the horse, physical (e.g. muscular) stiffness, or restrictions imposed by the rider. It is also embodied in the concept of 'free forward movement' whereby, once the horse has been given an aid to move forward in a particular gait, he continues to do so, with a minimum of 'reinforcing' aids, until asked to do something different. The presence of this quality is indicative that the horse has learnt to 'go forward from the leg' – the most fundamental requirement of a riding horse and the foundation for all subsequent training.

Regularity of gait is a matter of a repeated sequence of *correct* footfall, described in equestrian terminology as 'cadence'. It might be thought that, since there are accepted sequences for each gait (which could be considered as *defining* the gait), cadence would be automatic. In practice, however, this is frequently not the case. The following are simple examples of loss of cadence:

At walk, correct cadence is a regular 1.2.3.4 sequence of footfall. However, in some instances (for example, if the horse is hurried by the rider), there may be a tendency to group the lateral pairs of footfall more together, creating a 1,2...3,4 effect.

At trot, correct cadence exists when one diagonal pair of feet is placed on the ground together followed in regular sequence by the other pair. This sequence would generally be accepted not only as correct, but also as normal. However, in many cases, this is not precisely what happens; instead, on one or both diagonals, there may be two separate footfalls as opposed to one distinct 'beat'. Often, this double footfall will be virtually unnoticeable; in other cases, however, it may be quite distinct (and acknowledged by the dressage judge). Either way, there is, to some extent, a loss of cadence.

Canter is held to be a three-time gait; one hind foot strikes the ground, followed by the other hind foot and diagonally opposite forefoot together, and then the final forefoot. If this sequence is followed precisely and in regular time, the cadence will be correct. However, it is not that unusual for a horse to 'split the diagonal' (place the diagonal pair of feet to the ground separately – usually hind foot first). The resultant four-time or disunited canter shows an obvious loss of cadence.

It may be useful, at this juncture, to say a few words about 'rhythm'. This term is often used to describe regularity of gait and progression, and it may be that the reader is thinking that cadence and rhythm have the same meaning. However, while correctly cadenced gaits are certainly rhythmical, the presence of rhythm does not necessarily guarantee correct cadence. This is not pedantry, but a practical matter of which the thinking rider must be aware. To make a musical analogy, 4/4 time (four beats to the bar) is a perfectly good rhythm, but it is not the correct cadence for a (3/4) waltz.

Thus, if rhythm is defined as any regular pattern of time/stress, then it is quite possible that it may be present in any of the examples of *loss of cadence* given above. In each case, the time/stress pattern of footfall may be *regular*, but it is not *correct* for the gait concerned.

Regarding the use of 'rhythm' in describing regular progression (that is, over a succession of strides rather than within the stride itself), it is again, necessary to exercise caution. If a horse moves with even length and frequency of stride, his progress may be considered rhythmical. However, while any rhythmical progression might be regarded as superior to progress lacking in rhythm, the mere existence of rhythm does not guarantee that it will be 'good rhythm'. The horse may, for instance, move with a series of short, quick strides, 'scampering' along rather than propelling himself with power and grace. Alternatively, he may be sluggish and slow. In such cases, it is less likely that rhythm will be maintained but, where it does exist, it will not be proof that the horse is moving to optimum effect.

Having said this, it must be admitted that there is no absolute rule for assessing good rhythm of progression. One cannot, for instance, say that a horse of certain size displays good rhythm at trot when taking strides of x metres length at a frequency of y strides per minute. Horses are not production line machines, and such formulae would have little credibility. Instead, the quality of rhythmic progression will be assessed largely by reference to the *activity* shown by the horse, and this brings us to the next characteristic of correct training – the presence of impulsion.

IMPULSION In many respects, impulsion is the most important characteristic of correct training, its existence being a major factor in the presence and quality of the others. Impulsion is often defined as 'a desire to go forwards', and this is valuable both as a mental characteristic and for its physical manifestations. The basis of the latter is seen in increased activity of the hind limbs, which step purposefully forward beneath the horse (hocks 'active' or 'engaged') providing the foundation for correct movement.

There are various factors which help produce impulsion, the 'genuine article' being most usually observed in a horse who is fit, well, confident and enjoying his work. The physical manifestations can be produced to some extent by coercion (i.e. using artificial aids to reinforce the natural aids in stimulating the hind limbs), but the necessity to do so is really contrary to the definition of impulsion: the 'desire to go forward' should be for its own sake, not to avoid punishment for failing to do so. Furthermore, impulsion induced in this way is likely to be intermittent and short-lived, unless the horse is one of the 'lazy but honest' types who enjoys his work, but only after he has been woken up. The benefits of impulsion are:

1) It indicates a positive attitude in the horse.
2) Since the horse 'wants' to go forward, the rider will not need to spend time and effort in persuading him to do so, and can thus concentrate his energies in other directions.
3) Correct, active use of the hind limbs as the source of propulsion will promote and enhance quality of gaits, balance, correct outline, lightness, straightness and the ability to accept the aids.

This last point highlights the role of impulsion in enhancing the other characteristics of correct training and, as we examine them, it will become apparent that they follow on in something of a 'snowball' effect once impulsion is established.

LIGHTNESS This term refers to both lightness of the forehand and lightness of movement, the former being a prerequisite of the latter.

Lightness can only occur if the horse is moving actively from behind. Correct use of the hind limbs as the source of propulsion will free the forelimbs from any necessity to assist by 'pulling' the horse along, allowing them, instead, to fulfill their role of supporting and balancing the forehand.

The horse who *does* use his forelimbs to assist locomotion (the horse who is 'on the forehand') will usually carry his head and neck abnormally low and thrust forward, in an effort to balance himself and increase his 'pulling' power. He will therefore feel dull and heavy in the rider's hands ('leaning on the bit'), and convey a permanent impression that he is about to topple forwards. However, the horse who is moving correctly will be much better balanced; he will feel altogether lighter in the hands and the quality of movement will be enhanced, so that he will give an impression of floating or springing in his action, rather than lumbering, plodding or dragging himself along.

A further consequence of active use of the hind limbs is that it tends to promote a convex curvature of the horse's spinal column, so that he moves in a more 'rounded' outline. This allows for greater freedom of movement of the back muscles and, in the neck region, promotes a graceful curvature, with the joint beneath the poll relaxed, so that the head is carried naturally at an angle whereby the face is just a little in front of the vertical.

Although the precise outline will be dependent upon the horse's conformation and state of training, and the rider's intentions, it is this outline in general which best enables the rider to control the horse, and this brings us to the question of acceptance of aids.

ACCEPTANCE OF THE AIDS (SUBMISSION) It will be apparent by definition that the correctly trained horse will accept the aids – that is to say, he will respond positively to the rider's (properly applied) signals. However, the key words here are 'correctly trained' and 'accept'. Although the term 'submission' is often used to describe acceptance of the aids, it is important to bear in mind the objective of producing a state of *willing* obedience: the idea is to train the horse, not enslave him.

The ability of any horse to accept the aids is dependent upon the precepts that he both understand them, and is physically capable of responding as required.

With regard to the first factor, the aid applications acknowledged as correct in classical equitation have been developed logically with reference to the horse's mental processes and natural movement. This does not mean, however, that the aids will be automatically understood or accepted by a horse from the outset; rather, his understanding and acceptance will have to be developed by a system of progressive training. Regarding the horse's physical capacity to respond to the aids, it may simplify matters to look at this from two viewpoints – basic forward movement and general manoeuvrability.

Basic forward movement: While the principle of 'accepting the aids' applies to *all* the aids, the term is commonly used to refer primarily to the control of basic forward movement. This control is dependent upon two criteria: the ability to instigate forward movement, and the ability of the rider to mete it out according to his requirements. We have already established a progressive link through the concepts of free forward movement and impulsion, and seen that there is a consequent influence upon the development of lightness, and it is at this juncture that the very existence of correct forward movement can be seen to *assist* in its control. The reasons for this are:

1) Since the horse is moving in an athletic and balanced manner, he will have maximum control over his own movements, and thus have the maximum capacity to respond efficiently to the rider's signals.

2) Because of this, and because of the horse's willingness to move forwards, the rider will require only light application of the aids to encourage forward movement. This will not only make it easier to produce upward transitions/increase speed, but also to perform correct downward transitions/reduce speed, since the horse will move readily forward into the 'containing' rein contact.

3) We have seen that the horse who is exhibiting a degree of lightness will have a natural tendency to flex at the poll, and will also, by definition, be relatively 'light' in the rider's hands. These influences will greatly assist the rider in persuading the horse to accept the bit with a 'soft' contact.

Thus, while the rider cannot achieve total control over forward movement by the influences of seat and leg aids alone, their correct use will greatly assist in teaching the horse to respond to light, subtle applications of the rein aids, so that he moves willingly and obediently forward 'between leg and hand'.

Manoeuvrability: This is not a recognised dressage term, but is used here to describe the horse's capacity to respond accurately to aids concerned with changes of direction. There are two influences which affect his abilities in this respect: 'straightness' and suppleness.

Straightness of a horse is a quality which is not confined to his moving correctly along a straight line. It includes the concept of the hind feet stepping into the tracks of the forefeet whether he is moving straight forwards or travelling on a circle. In the case of 'lateral' movements, where the feet follow different tracks, straightness implies that the horse maintains the desired direction of travel with the tracks of the feet remaining parallel.

Straightness is obviously a desirable characteristic in any horse, but it becomes essential if a horse is to perform well in

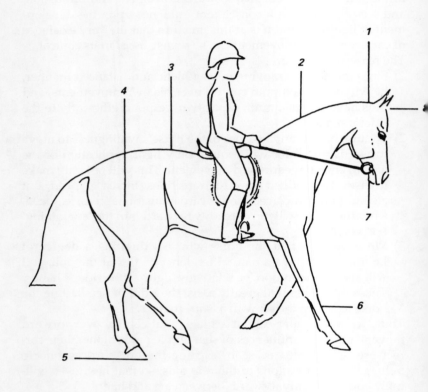

Characteristics of training: Correct

1 *Poll highest point and flexed;* **2** *Muscular development of topline of neck;*
3 *Supple 'rounded' outline of back;* **4** *Hindquarters 'engaged';* **5** *Hind limbs
stepping actively 'underneath' horse;* **6** *Light, free movement of forehand;*
7 *Lower jaw flexed. Horse 'accepting' bit;* **8** *Happy demeanour*

dressage tests since, without it, there is no chance of movements
being performed with real accuracy. Unfortunately, very few
horses are naturally 'straight'; most tend (like humans) to be
slightly asymmetrical in conformation, and thus show 'left-' or
'right-handed' preferences. It is, therefore, necessary for the

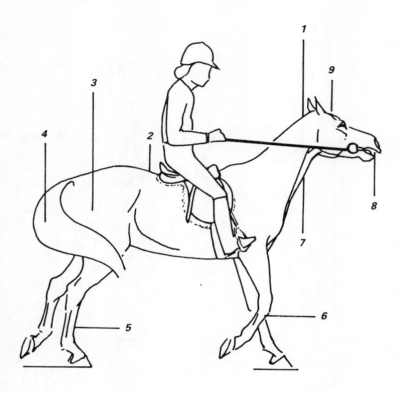

Characteristics of training: Incorrect

1 *Stiffness of poll*; **2** *Hollow, stiff outline of back*; **3** *Hindquarters inactive*; **4** *Swishing tail denoting resistance*; **5** *Hind limbs trailing*; **6** *Forehand heavy 'dragging' horse along*; **7** *Muscular development of underside of neck*; **8** *Mouth open/jaw crossed, horse 'resisting' rein contact*; **9** *Unhappy demeanour*

trainer/rider to remedy this lack of straightness, the degree to which he can do so depending, to some extent, upon the underlying causes. If, for instance, the horse is suffering from some congenital deformity, it is unlikely that remedial riding will effect a cure – although it may minimise the effects. In most cases,

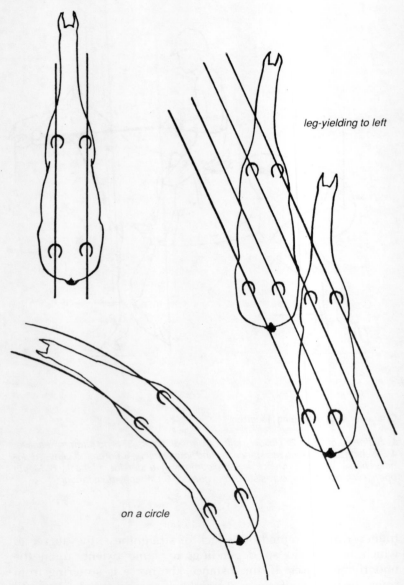

on a straight line

leg-yielding to left

on a circle

Examples of correct alignment: ('straightness')

however, the horse can be made straight (or at least a good deal straighter) by the intelligent use of suppling exercises.

These exercises embrace the apparent paradox that straightness can be enhanced by improving the horse's ability to bend. The explanation for this is that most crookedness is rooted in muscular and/or joint stiffness on one side of the horse, and suppling exercises are designed to remedy this situation. If, for instance, a horse has relatively weak muscles on one side and strong, stiff muscles on the other, he will tend to be crooked towards his weak side and find it difficult to bend the other way. In order to straighten him, it will be necessary to place emphasis upon exercises which will help to supple the stiff muscles and strengthen the weak ones. Once this has been achieved, equal emphasis must be placed on keeping both sides of the horse in supple condition, so that the potential for straightness is maintained.

The classic suppling exercise is shoulder-in, but its effectiveness is dependent both upon the rider being sufficiently experienced to ask for, and recognise it correctly, and the horse's general training being of such a level that he is capable of responding. Until these criteria can be met, attempts to ride the movement will prove fruitless, and it is wiser in such circumstances to concentrate upon obtaining correct bend on turns, circles and serpentines (the emphasis being on bending towards the stiff side).

Since, by their nature, suppling exercises require the horse to perform movements which he will find difficult, his ability and desire to respond to the aids must be constantly at the forefront of the rider's mind. While it is almost inevitable that some degree of resistance will be offered at times, this can be minimised by the rider not demanding too much at once, and overcome by reasonable insistence and repetition. The exercises should be performed frequently and fairly intensely, but only for short periods, and they should be interspersed with plenty of active straight line work, and movements ridden on the horse's 'good' rein. The intention must be that there is sufficient effort to make progress, but not so much that serious resistances and evasions are provoked, or strain/injury occurs. (In this context it is important – especially with young horses – that too much work on tight circles is avoided, as this can overtax the joints.)

Regarding work on straight lines, it is important that this is recognised as complementary to, and not merely a relief from, the suppling exercises themselves. Straight line work allows the hip and shoulder joints on both sides of the horse equal freedom of movement, thus helping to improve gait purity, and assists in stabilising the centres of gravity and motion (which will destabilise if the horse leans/tilts through turns), thereby improving balance.

Furthermore, since the horse is designed, first and foremost, to move forwards, he will most readily generate impulsion when moving in a straight line. This must be encouraged between exercises requiring lateral bend in order to ensure that the horse is using his hind limbs actively *before* he is asked to perform such exercises. This will improve the quality and usefulness of the exercises, and help prevent evasions rooted in inactivity.

LOOSENESS This term is being used increasingly in dressage jargon, and is now one of the factors considered when collective marks are awarded for certain tests.

Its use in Britain seems to have resulted from a rather inadequate translation of a German 'umbrella' expression (*Losgelassenheit*), intended to describe an absence of mental or physical tension. Such absence of tension is undoubtedly desirable in the horse, but the use of the word 'looseness' to describe it is rather confusing and unsatisfactory, since too many of the English definitions/synonyms are inappropriate descriptions of what is intended. For instance, a judge is unlikely to favour a horse for exhibiting laxity of bowels or morals during a test, neither will he give extra marks to one whose joints dislocate.

A study of the various indications of 'looseness' listed by European writers suggests that they can be more precisely defined by familiar terms such as 'calm', 'supple', 'flexible', 'ease of movement', 'lack of resistance' etc. It is suggested, therefore, that the reader continues to think in such terms, so that he is not confused or persuaded into believing that there is any virtue in allowing the horse to flop around the arena like a sack of blancmange.

3
The Rider's Role

In addition to being *aware* of the objects and principles of dressage, it is necessary for the rider himself to perform in such a way that he enhances, rather than inhibits, the characteristics of correct training. This fact will, of course, be especially significant for the owner-rider but, as far as performing a dressage test is concerned, it applies equally to the rider sitting on an unknown hireling for a total period of twenty minutes.

While it is always *desirable* to ride any horse to the best of one's ability, it could be argued that, in some equestrian activities, it may not be absolutely essential to do so. However, as far as riding a dressage test is concerned, any approach other than a determination to do one's best renders the exercise completely pointless. No horse will go better than he is ridden and, since the object of a dressage test is to show off the horse's training to best effect, a rider who does not *try* to achieve the best possible result is wasting his time on the animal's back.

Let us, therefore, look at the rider's role from both a physical and mental viewpoint, and examine how he is able to influence the characteristics of correct training.

The Physical Aspect

While it is not the main purpose of this book to discuss the technical/mechanical aspects of posture and aid applications in detail, these factors are obviously of fundamental importance in riding dressage. It may, therefore, be worthwhile reiterating the basic elements, and the reasons for their desirability. (These matters are dealt with at greater length in another book in this series – *Riding From Scratch*).

31

POSTURE It must be borne in mind that the riding posture recognised as classically 'correct' is not so recognised merely because it looks good, but because it is mechanically efficient. The key elements of this efficiency are:

1) Rider security.
2) The placing of the rider in a position of harmony and balance with the horse (which of itself promotes rider security).
3) The placing of the rider in a position from which the aids can be applied effectively.

Logic dictates that departures from correct posture will, to a greater or lesser extent, detract from at least one, and probably all, of these elements. In brief, the main points of correct posture are:

Seat (i.e. upper thighs, buttocks, pelvis, lower back). Thigh muscles flat against the saddle, 'holding' but not gripping fiercely; backside in lowest part of the saddle; rider sitting on his seatbones (the base of each side of the pelvis) with equal weight distribution on each, and over as large an area of the seatbones as possible; lower back braced just sufficiently to ensure correct base for erect upper body.

Upper body: Still and upright (though not tense and stiff) posture emenating from correctly aligned spine and elevated rib cage; rider looking straight ahead.

Legs: Insides of thighs, knees, calves and ankles resting flat against the horse, with toes pointing straight forwards. Natural, not forced, flexion of knee and ankle joints. Lower legs (except when giving specific aids which require leg to slide back) remaining against the girth, with ankle joint vertically beneath both hip and shoulder.

Hands (and arms): Upper arms hanging down naturally from still shoulders; straight line through elbow/forearm/wrist/rein/bit; hands width of horse's mouth (or slightly more) apart (approx. 12-15cm); hands level with thumbs uppermost; backs of hands (as a 'norm') appearing as extensions of forearms (i.e. not 'curled').

Departures from correct posture can be broadly categorised into those which result in the rider tipping forward, backward or sideways.

If the rider tips forward, the security of his seat will be weakened, and the ability of the seat to absorb the effects of the horse's motion will be impaired, as will the ability to apply

— *The Rider's Role* —

effective seat and back aids. There will be a tendency to try to improve security by using the legs to grip, and this will adversely affect the application of correct leg aids.

Tipping backwards may place the rider's weight behind the horse's centre of motion, producing a permanent crude 'driving' aid which can provoke a hollow outline of the horse's back. This will be aggravated by a tendency to hang on with the reins and to thrust the legs forward, which, again, will impair the effective applications of leg aid, thus further aggravating any hollowness of outline.

Tipping sideways (sitting crooked) will unbalance the horse laterally, and cause him to try to step underneath the heavier side of the rider, thereby producing crookedness.

In their more extreme forms, these errors may render the rider incapable of any significant degree of control, but it should be noted that even experienced, competent riders can easily lapse into lesser errors *of the same type*. It is, therefore, important that the rider who wishes to get the best from his horse pays constant attention to his own posture; the benefits of competent instruction being self-evident in this respect.

AIDS AND THEIR APPLICATION   The term 'aids' is commonly used to describe both the agencies by which the rider communicates with the horse, and the specific signals sent via these lines of communication. It is important that the rider understands the needs to keep the lines of communication open at all times, but it is also important that he gives specific signals only as and when appropriate. There is a fundamental need to be constantly in touch with the horse, but nothing will be gained by overloading the communication system with a stream of repetitive, contradictory or confusing commands.

The benefits of the aids which are considered classically correct are that they are simple, they have direct, logical links to the horse's psychology and physiology, and they can be applied from the saddle without disturbing the rider's basic posture or balance.

It will do no harm to remind ourselves of the basic functions of the individual aids:

The legs initiate, maintain or increase forward movement and play a major role in producing and controlling lateral bend and direction. They remain in communication with the horse by resting lightly against his sides, and give specific signals by sliding along his flanks and being applied (singly or in pairs as appropriate) with varying degrees of inward pressure.

The hands provide, via reins and bit, a 'point of reference' at the front of the horse, they mete out the forward movement instigated by the rider's legs, and they guide the forehand in unison with the directional aids/bend produced in the horse by the leg aids. The hands remain in communication with the horse by maintaining a rein contact, and they influence the forward movement by increasing the contact ('containing') or lightening it ('allowing') as required. As directional aids, they simply 'ask' the horse to look in the required direction, and allow him to do so; they are never correctly used to 'steer' or pull the horse's forehand round.

The seat. Once the rider is sufficiently experienced and practised to use the seat effectively as a stabliser and shock absorber, he can begin to employ it to produce either a 'driving' or 'holding' effect, and also to influence the horse by subtle variations in weight distribution. The former effects are produced by bracing the lower back to various degrees. Given that the rider's spine will be pretty much vertically above the horse's centre of motion, this bracing will produce a forward driving effect, normally employed in conjunction with the leg aids. Applying such aids while 'allowing' the horse forwards with the hands will result in increased forward movement, while applying them in conjunction with a 'containing' rein contact will produce a greater steadying effect than would result from 'leg into hand' alone. Slight alterations in weight distribution between the seatbones can supplement other directional aids, in fact experienced riders may apply such aids almost subconsciously. However, it is very important that such redistribution of weight is confined to the seat itself, and does not entail any leaning/collapsing of the upper body.

The voice can be used to soothe, encourage or reprimand the horse, but any usage during a dressage test will be penalised by the loss of two marks on each occasion.

Artificial aids. In the context of dressage tests these are limited to whip and spurs, whose purposes are to supplement/heighten the effect of the leg aids. Although it is always preferable to obtain the desired results by sole use of the natural aids, the dressage rider should be prepared to use whip or spur (correctly) when he considers that they will produce an improved response from the horse. It is, for instance, much better (and will look better to the judge) to make occasional use of these aids to maintain activity in the horse rather than to bang and nag away fruitlessly with the legs. However, over-reliance upon, or inappropriate use of the artificial aids is to be avoided. Such actions constitute bad equestrian practice, and will not impress the judge with either the horse's training or the rider's competence.

The principles of correct aid applications are that they should be as light and sparing *as is effective*, and they should be applied in harmonious combinations, with the horse being ridden from the hindquarters forward. This means that, in all circumstances, forward movement – or the desire to move forwards – should be first encouraged, and then channeled as appropriate in order that the required response is produced. This principle lies at the root of the common adages 'leg before hand' and 'ride leg into hand'. It has been said that 'in the art of riding, nothing is invariably right or invariably wrong' (Waldemar Seunig). However, if there is an inviolate law of equitation, then riding from the hindquarters forward is surely it.

The Mental Aspect

Even if we assume that the term 'technique' not only describes a rider's physical actions, but also implies an understanding of their physiological effects upon the horse, technique alone is still not enough to make a truly effective rider. We have already touched upon this point by considering the aids not as push-button signals, but as *communications* with the horse. Effective communication involves such qualities as 'feel', rapport and sympathy, and these will be enhanced if the rider has the imagination to 'think like a horse'. Furthermore, communication being a two-way process, they will help the rider to interpret the signals sent by the horse who, as a sentient creature, will continually emit indications as to whether he is finding the rider's requirements of him easy, enjoyable, difficult, irritating, confusing and so forth. Whilst it is not suggested that such indications should prompt the rider to indulge the horse's every whim, an ability to receive and evaluate them will help the rider to tailor his own communications so that they become more acceptable and effective. This is of particular importance to the dressage rider, whose true role is to educate the horse, rather than to wring a short-term result from him by any available expedient.

Horses, like people, respond best to an educational process which is sympathetic, consistent, presented in terms they understand, and shows a steady, logical progression. In contrast, 'bodges', short-cuts and work executed under coercion stick out like a sore thumb in the dressage arena. If the rider is to pursue the former course, one of his greatest assets will be patience. By this, we do not mean an interminable acceptance of lack of progress, but the ability to take a deep breath and evaluate the situation calmly when things go wrong, rather than to react irrationally through irritation or loss of temper. Riding in general, and individual horses in particular, can be enormously frustrating, and there must be very few riders who can honestly claim never to have 'lost their cool'. However, even if we can sometimes sympathise with such reactions, they can never be condoned since – even leaving aside consideration for the horse – they invariably aggravate the problem.

One of the acid tests of true horsemanship is the speed and accuracy with which a rider can assess a problem and start to remedy it, and no-one can gain this ability without being prepared to 'listen' to the horse's responses.

Of course, there may be times when a difficulty arises through blatant disobedience on the horse's part and, in such circumstances, it is quite legitimate to act by correcting, reprimanding or even punishing him. However, in order for such action to be just and constructive, it is necessary for the rider to be certain that sheer disobedience *is* the cause (that is to say the horse shows reluctance to do something of which he is *known* to be capable), and that there are no abnormal circumstances (physical discomfort/illness/fright etc.) involved.

It has to be said, however, that most problems and 'disobediences' originate from some form of rider error, be it of posture, aid application or judgement (e.g. wrong assessment of a horse's level of training/understanding). It is, therefore, most important that, when assessing any difficulty, the rider starts by looking at

himself as the most likely cause. It is a salutary lesson that the more
experienced and talented a rider becomes, the less ready he will be
to blame problems upon actual disobedience on the horse's part.

Rider Influences Upon the Characteristics of Training

Having looked in general terms at the physical and mental
aspects of riding, we can now consider how the rider can use his
skill and understanding to enhance the characteristics of correct
training. At the same time we should bear in mind the reverse
side of the coin, and remind ourselves of those actions and errors
which will impair the horse's way of going, to the detriment of
his training and the rider's dressage score.

GAIT QUALITY

Positive rider influences:

Good posture

Recognising good natural gaits,
and avoiding disturb-ing them.

Correct aid applications when
asking for transitions and gait
variants.

Recognising poor cadence and
rhythm and seeking to improve
them – initially by asking for
increased activity of hind limbs.

Recognising deficiencies in gait
quality arising from defects in conformation or past training, and
seeking to remedy/alleviate them.
Specific problems (especially congenital defects) may largely dictate
the scope for improvement. In
some cases, improvement may be
possible only through long-term
ministrations of a highly experi-

Negative rider influences:

Bad posture/postural errors in
general

Disturbing good natural gaits, e.g.
by hurrying horse into taking short,
quick steps/ stirdes or discourag-
ing forward movement by over-
restrictive rein aids and/or lack of
support from legs.

Incorrect aid applications when
asking for transitions and gait
variants.

Failure to identify poor cadence
and rhythm, thus allowing further
degeneration.

Failure to identify such gait defects
or, worse still, riding/schooling in
a manner likely to aggravate them.

WARNING: unskilled lungeing, or
lungeing without attention to
detail or purpose, is likely to do
more harm than good.

enced trainer/rider. In others, marked improvement may result from adherence to correct basics (e.g. plenty of active straight line work to alleviate 'dishing' or 'plaiting' caused through lack of condition or incorrect lungeing, rather than through joint malformation).

IMPULSION
Positive rider influences:
Encouraging the presence of factors likely to produce a natural 'desire to go forwards', i.e. attention to horse's well-being and comfort, promoting confidence in rider and enjoyment of work (assisted by variety).

Riding the horse from the hindquarters forward i.e. encouraging the physical manifestations of impulsion and using them as a basis upon which to build control.

In the sluggish/lazy horse, inducing greater activity – if necessary, by supplementing natural aids with correct use of artificial aids.
(As we have seen, ideal, true impulsion is largely a gift from the horse himself. However, the physical manifestations of impulsion are so crucial to correct movement that is is better to induce them than to try and ride a horse from whom they are absent).

Negative rider influences:
Neglect of horse's well-being and comfort, generally bad riding, impatience, punishing horse in the mouth, inducing staleness/boredom by overwork/repetition.

Riding the horse 'on the hands' i.e. restricting/discouraging forward movement, aids originating in 'pulling' hands.
Under-riding – asking too little of the horse, thereby dulling his enthusiasm, concentration, confidence in, and respect for, the rider.

Accepting sluggishness/inactivity. Abuse of aids in attempting to create activity. (If a horse need 'beating up' to make him go forward then either the rider is doing something drastically wrong, or else there are severe deficiencies in the horse's condition or training).

LIGHTNESS Since lightness will only occur if the horse is moving with impulsion, it follows that the rider influences mentioned above will apply. As far as the horse feeling 'light in the hand' is concerned, it is important to understand that this will not result merely from the rider taking a light hold of the reins; it is a quality of the balanced, responsive horse – not a result of a passive rider.

ACCEPTANCE OF AIDS

Positive rider influences:	*Negative rider influences:*
	General
Correct posture.	Postural errors.
Understanding the reasons behind various aids applications (i.e. how they relate to horse's physiology and psychology).	Ignorance of same.
Considering the aids as communications, and tailoring aid applications in the light of the horse's responses.	Considering the aids solely in terms of push-button commands, and applying them in this manner regardless of horse's responses.

Specially relating to control of forward movement

Riding the horse forward into acceptable rein contact.	Actively or passively discouraging forward movement.
Sensitive hands (hands which will 'soften' contact once horse has responded to a 'containing' rein aid).	Heavy hands provoking resistances.
The feel and ability to vibrate the bit gently in the horse's mouth as and when the occasion requires.	'Dead' hands (hands which do nothing but hold the reins). 'Sawing' with the hands (pulling the bit around in the horse's mouth as opposed to vibrating it).

Specially relating to control of straightness

On a straight line: Positive awareness of intended line of travel.	Vagueness about same.
Symmetrical aid applications.	Asymmetrical aid applications.

Encouraging active forward movement to promote balance and gait purity.	Hindering active forward movement, provoking loss of straightness through resistance/loss of balance.
Early discernment and correction of incipient loss of straightness mainly through seat and leg aids.	Late reaction to actual loss of straightness; attempts at correction mainly through rein aids.
On turns and circles: Accurate mental picture of position, size and shape.	Vagueness regarding same.
Maintenance of impulsion and rhythm.	Loss of impulsion and rhythm.
Correct, harmonious combination of aids to ride 'whole of horse' onto required circle/arc (i.e. correct bend).	Concentrating upon 'steering' horse's forehand with the reins, e.g. pulling horse's head round with inside rein, creating too much bend in neck and encouraging/provoking hindquarters to escape/swing outside circumference of circle. Trying to hold horse out on circle with outside rein, creating wrong bend and destroying shape of circle.

4

The Dressage Arena

Since all dressage tests are described in terms of the standard marker letters around the arena, it is a pre-requisite of both learning and riding the test that the rider is completely familiar with the arena layout.

All the preliminary level, and novice *horse trial* tests are ridden in a 40m × 20m arena. The majority of teaching arenas conform to these dimensions, and are marked out accordingly, the markers being used to direct movements during lessons. It is probable, therefore, that most riders will be reasonably familiar with the positioning of the markers by the time they start to ride tests – but it is worthwhile ensuring that this 'reasonable familiarity' is converted to certain knowledge; there is nothing worse than knowing, in mid-test, that you have to canter at H, and having a complete mental block as to where on earth H is.

For those who do not normally ride in a marked arena (or who have navigated their way through lessons by the expedient of following the rider in front!) there is an old mnemonic which helps one recall the clockwise sequence of the perimeter markers: All King Edward's Horses Can Manage Big Fences (A,K,E,H,C,M,B,F).

Once the rider progresses beyond preliminary level, he may encounter tests designed to be ridden in a long (60m × 20m) arena. This applies to three of the novice tests currently in use (1994), Numbers 16, 18 and 19. In the long arena, the perimeter markers used in the short arena remain in the same sequence, the quarter markers (K,H,M,F) remain six metres from the corners, and markers E and B are still the mid-points on the long sides. However, the arena is elongated by increasing the distance from the quarter markers to E and B, and four extra perimeter markers

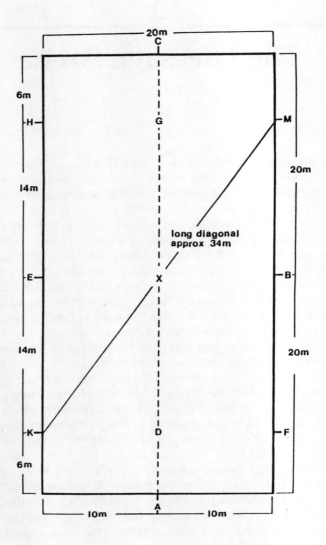

Short dressage arena (40m × 20m)

— *The Dressage Arena* —

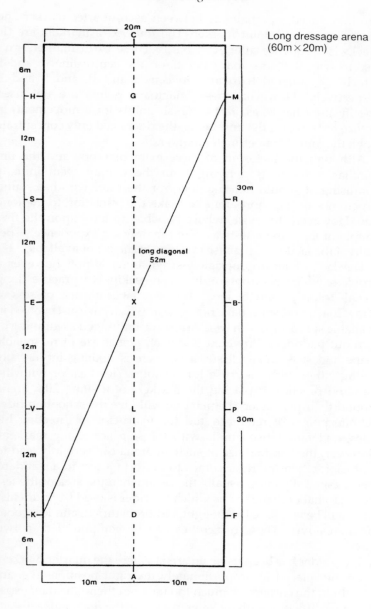

Long dressage arena
(60m × 20m)

43

are introduced, one halfway between each quarter marker and the adjacent mid-point marker. The four extra markers are (in clockwise sequence after K) V,S,R,P. These extra markers give rise to two new imaginary points on the centre line, L and I, which are situated halfway between V and P, and S and R respectively. However, these imaginary points are not used specifically (that is, as start or finish points for a movement) in novice tests, so, for the time being, the rider need only concentrate upon the four extra perimeter markers.

Although the inclusion of these extra markers, and the unfamiliar movements deriving from them, may seem initially confusing, it should not take long for the rider who has sound experience of the short arena to make the transition to the long one. However, it is wise, where possible, to look upon the first couple of long arena tests as being mainly for experience, especially if the facility to practise in a long arena is not available.

The lack of an appropriately-sized arena is not, however a problem which confronts only those seeking to practise 'long arena' tests. Although most riding establishments possess a 40m × 20m arena, some have riding areas which have just evolved in available space, or which were originally envisaged as jumping or turn-out paddocks. Provided that such arenas are of reasonable shape and size, and well surfaced, there is nothing intrinscially wrong either with their use for schooling/lessons, or with the common practice of placing the markers of a 40m × 20m arena around their perimeter; the markers will give the schooling rider definite points of reference, aid the instructor in directing his rides, and familiarise pupils with the *sequence* of the markers. However, the habitual use of such an arena can certainly lead to confusion when the rider comes to perform a test in a standard arena, especially (as is usually the case) when the area of the test arena is smaller than the one which the rider is used to. Suddenly, there will be less time for thought and preparation, and less room for manoeuvre. These difficulties can be compounded in two ways:

1) If the rider has been using an arena where the quarter markers are not placed in proportionately the right positions (i.e. are right in the corners, or much too far from them), he may experience difficulty with movements across the diagonals.

2) By the tendency of instructors in non-standard arenas to give

commands as though they *were* in a standard arena. For instance, an instructor in an arena which may be 30 metres wide might give the command 'ride a 20 metre circle from E', when he actually intends the pupil to ride a circle the full width of the arena: the pupil who actually rides a 20 metre circle being admonished for not reaching the opposite track. The effects of such slack terminology increase where tighter movements are involved, and the rider used to performing '10 metre circles' which are really 15 metres in diameter may have real difficulty in making the turns onto and from the centre line which are a feature of most tests.

There is a final, slightly ironic problem of dimensions which may occur if a rider frequents an establishment which does possess a 60m × 20m arena, and he uses it to practise a short arena test. It is quite feasible to adapt most short arena tests to the long arena – the extra markers are simple ignored – but this obviously allows a misleading amount of time and room on the long sides and diagonals. The expedient of partitioning off one end of the arena at the SR or VP line pretty much solves the problem of length, but creates an asymmetrical arena with one set of quarter markers well out of place.

If the rider is a non-owner who hires horses from a commercial establishment, it may be that he will have little choice or control over these difficulties of non-standard arenas. In such circumstances, however, it is helpful to be fully aware of the situation, so that one is at least forewarned that there will be differences in the test arena, even if one's practical experience of the differences is limited.

5

Movements in Preliminary and Novice Dressage Tests

It is important to understand that the performance of any specific movement is not, of itself, a primary objective of dressage. One does not, for instance, 'teach a horse dressage' by taking him into the school and deciding at random to attempt half-pass or to impose a certain head carriage. Such an approach will, at best, produce crude, forced approximations of the desired effects, and is more likely to detract from the horse's training than enhance it.

A horse's ability to move correctly in a certain manner or outline will arise progressively from correct training, and thus the various movements performed in dressage tests should be considered as demonstrative of that training, and not as isolated ends in themselves. The series of dressage tests produced by the B.H.S. Dressage Group is intended to reflect this principle. The tests are grouped into various 'levels', and tests within each level include only movements which a horse undergoing correct and progressive training might be expected to perform at that juncture. The levels start with 'preliminary', and range through 'novice', 'elementary', 'medium' and 'advanced medium' to 'advanced'. A separate series of tests exists for use in horse trials, and these tests take account of the fact that the horses performing them are not dressage 'specialists'; for instance, the tests used in 'advanced' horse trials are of broadly 'medium' (dressage) standard.

For the purposes of this book, we shall consider the movements required at preliminary and novice (including novice horse trial) level, since these are the standards suited to, and used at, club and local level competitions, where relatively inexperienced horses and riders are being catered for. Readers with aspirations beyond these levels should bear in mind the progressive nature of training, and the corollary that success at a more advanced level must invariably be built upon the foundation of correct basics. The number of different movements used in preliminary and novice level tests is actually quite low; variety in the tests resulting largely from altering the sequence and location of movements. The movements outlined below are extracted from the tests 'current' in 1994 (that is, those for use in official competitions under B.H.S. Dressage Group rules in that year) – however, they comprise the core of movements upon which all tests at preliminary and novice level are based – including the older tests which are still frequently used for club events.

Preliminary Level Tests

GAITS The gaits themselves do not actually constitute movements of the test but the various movements are ridden as specified in the gaits below. The quality of the gaits will be constantly assessed by the judge, and will influence both the mark awarded for each movement and the collective mark given at the end of each test. Therefore, although the first objective is to perform movements in the prescribed gaits, the rider must also be concerned with gait quality. The attitude 'it says trot and we're trotting' is not the prescription for success.

Medium walk: Virtually all movements in walk are to be performed at medium walk. This requires energetic, active but unhurried movement, with the horse taking somewhat longer strides than he might if walking naturally round the field. The increased stride length is characterised by the horse overtracking a little – that is to say that his hind feet should step a little (one or two hoof lengths) beyond the prints made by his forefeet. Obviously, the rider cannot see whether his horse is overtracking, but he should be able to feel whether or not he is moving purposefully forward, and act accordingly. Increased activity at walk can usually be obtained by sitting deep with a slightly braced back and applying light leg pressure in rhythm with the horse's movement. However the rider should not attempt to 'row' the horse along with his upper body and kicking or nagging at the horse with repeated prods from the heels will either be ignored, evaded (by a shortlived surge) or provoke the horse into bustling along with short quick steps and loss of cadence.

Free walk on a long rein: This will demonstrate whether the horse will remain in balance and obedient to the aids when the rein support lessens. The rider continues to ask the horse to move actively forward, and gradually and smoothly allows the reins to lengthen. The horse should continue to walk out at least to the extent of 'tracking up' (hind feet stepping into the prints of the forefeet), and should stretch his neck gently forward and down, and relax his jaw. Tipping onto the forehand, breaking into trot or ignoring the offer to stretch are all indications of training deficiencies. The rider can help his cause by sensitivity in 'offering' and 'allowing' the rein to the horse, and by keeping a light, but definite contact (the requirement is for a long rein, not a loose rein). Conversely, a sudden abandonment of the reins and a dig in the horse's ribs will not help at the best of times, and will certainly exaggerate any of the problems described above. It is worth nothing that the instruction 'free walk on a long rein' is often followed *immediately* by an instruction for medium walk, or even a change of gait (e.g. 'HXF change rein at a free walk on a long rein, F working trot'). It is not feasible to make such a change abruptly and well, so, in the last few strides of free walk, the rider must gently and smoothly re-establish rein length and the appropriate contact. Here again, a sudden snatching up of the reins is not conducive to good results, sensitivity being the order of the day.

Working trot: The horse should track-up and move with a pleasant degree of activity, this gait representing the natural stride length and movement of a horse of reasonable conformation and balance. Under Riding Club, Pony Club and Dressage Group rules (at this level), the rider is at liberty to rise or sit, and, as in the school, his choice will be largely a matter of how he wishes to influence the horse. In rising trot, it is politic to be on the diagonal usually accepted as correct – i.e. to sit as the horse's outside forefoot and inside hind foot touch the ground. This can be determined by sight – the rider sitting as the horse's inside shoulder moves forward – but it is recommended that riders learn to 'feel' the diagonal rather than having to look for it.

Working canter: The canter equivalent of the working trot. It is essential that all canter work be performed on the correct 'lead'; incorrect lead (wrong leg) being marked down very severely – however exemplary the counter-canter! Failure to recognise/

48

correct a wrong lead will also detract from the collective marks awarded to the rider.

TRANSITIONS As with the gaits, transitions can be considered constituent parts of the movements – many movements starting and/or finishing with a transition. In most instances, the transition is required *at* a prescribed marker (i.e. when the rider is level with the marker), and early or late transitions are penalised, thus placing extra emphasis upon the general requirement to think ahead and prepare.

At the levels under discussion, downward transitions may be progressive (e.g. trot to halt may be ridden via a few intermediate strides of walk). In some instances the tests will make specific provision for this by actually stipulating a short period of the intermediate gait. However, where progressive transitions are optional, their choice may make the rider's role technically easier, but will tend to place greater emphasis upon the need to think ahead, in order to ensure that the transition does not include an unnecessary amount of the intermediate gait and that it is completed at the prescribed marker.

Regarding upward transitions; these should all be direct although again, this is often allowed for by the tests stipulating changes gait by gait. However, it should be particularly noted that the halt to trot transition common to most tests should be ridden as prescribed.

On those occasions when it is stipulated only that a transition be performed *between* markers, the alert rider can make good use of the leeway provided. This condition is usually applied to transitions to or from canter, and these are normally performed in a corner of the arena (e.g. 'between C and H, working canter'). The optimum time to ask for such a transition is halfway through the corner when, if the aids to go through the corner have been correctly applied, and the horse is correctly bent, the rider need do little but squeeze with his legs. If he possess sufficient 'feel' to know when the horse's outside hind leg is stepping forwards beneath him, and applies the canter aid at the moment, then he has a chance of obtaining an excellent transition. The more experienced rider will probably – consciously or subconsciously – wait for this moment before giving the aid.

The period of grace between the two markers can also be

usefully employed to improve the trot before asking for the canter. (The rider should, of course, already have prepared, but, in this instance, he has an additional chance). If the horse is running along on his forehand, a subtle half-halt going into the corner can work wonders, rebalancing him before the transition is requested. In a similar, if more crucial, vein, the opportunity exists for a second attempt to obtain canter should the first fail. If the horse 'hangs fire', the rider should keep calm, wait a moment, then reapply the aids firmly but correctly. Should the horse respond to the first aids not by ignoring them, but by trotting faster, the use of a half-halt before reapplying the aids is, again, indicated. Even if this results in the transition being late, it represents a better chance of success than a panic-stricken fusillade of Thelwellesque urgings. (If the rider has prior knowledge of potential problems with canter transitions, it may be appropriate to ask for canter at the earliest permissible moment, to allow more room for manoeuvre.)

Another potential use for the room between markers is to improve any deficiencies in lateral bend in the horse by pushing him into the corner with the inside leg, whilst 'holding' the quarters with the outside leg. This is most important because asking for a canter lead when the horse is incorrectly bent may create various difficulties (wrong lead being the major one), and is most unlikely to result in a good transition.

In those cases where downward transitions can be ridden between markers, it makes sense to time the aids with the intention of getting the transition just after the first marker. This allows some leeway if the horse is a little unbalanced or resistant; alternatively, if the transition is smooth and prompt, it gives the rider a little more time to think ahead to the next movement.

Notwithstanding the requirement for accuracy, there is also considerable emphasis placed upon the quality of transitions, and it should be noted that, in general, smooth transitions performed slightly early or late will be better regarded than rough, abrupt ones performed bang on the marker. Since bad transitions are not only undesirable in themselves, but also affect the ensuing movement, the general rule is – don't panic!

THE HALT   The halt is, effectively, another transition, which poses further problems in that any defect will be frozen before the judge's eyes. A correct halt will be: accurate (in the right place), straight (on the intended line), square (hind feet, forefeet and lateral pairs parallel), and established (indicated by a distinct period of stillness – four seconds being regarded as the 'norm'). The horse should remain attentive – that is to say, ready to move off promptly upon command – but he should not fret or fidget.

In order to achieve a good halt, the rider must follow the principles outlined for aid applications and transitions; he must take special care to apply the aids symmetrically, and to ride 'leg and seat into hand'. Once the halt is established, leg and rein contact should be eased slightly, but neither must be lost.

One of the main problems with halt lies in its stationary nature. If a rider feels he has made a bad transition from one gait to another, he may curse inwardly, but the moment has passed. At halt, however, there is a tremendous temptation to try and remedy deficiencies which may be embarrassingly apparent. In most cases, it is best to resist such temptation, since 'fiddling about' usually makes matters worse. There are two main reasons for this: firstly, lack of actual forward movement works against the rider and, secondly, there is a chance that the horse may misinterpret any improvised aids as being signals to move forwards/rein-back/turn on the forehand.

If, then, the rider can perceive any incipient crookedness or a trailing leg as he asks for a halt, he has a moment in which to attempt correction. Once the horse has stopped, however, the least harmful course of action is to grin (or grimace) and bear it.

THE SALUTE The salute is basically an acknowledgement of the judge, but also serves to show that the rider has control of the halt. Salutes form part of each test, being performed if there is an initial halt on the centre line and, in each case, during the final halt. The salute is an integral part of the test and, if it is omitted or performed incorrectly, the error will be reflected in the score for the movement. There are two accepted methods of saluting:
1) The traditional method for gentlemen – whip and reins taken in left hand, right hand removes hat and lowers it to rider's side, rider inclines head, replaces hat, retakes reins.
2) For ladies, or anyone wearing a hat with chin harness – whip and reins taken in left hand, right arm down by side, rider

inclines head, retakes reins.
The salute should commence after the halt has been established,
and be completed before the horse is asked to move off.

FIGURES The figures of the test consist of straight lines, circles
or part circles, and combinations thereof. Correct shape and
accurate location are of fundamental importance, and it is worth
considering these basically simple constituents in some detail.
Straight lines: These *must be* straight, and must start and finish at
the prescribed markers. Movements which traverse a short side
of the arena should – at walk and trot at any rate – include some
straight line work (as opposed to being ridden as continual
curves/arcs).

Lines across the long diagonals (e.g. from K to M) must start
and finish at the appropriate markers; they should not be ridden
from corner to corner. To cross a diagonal correctly, the rider
should be thinking ahead, and prepared to use the aids correctly
to guide the whole length of the horse smoothly onto the
proposed line of travel. Common errors are: getting to the first
marker and tugging on the inside rein, or allowing the horse to
fall through the preceding corner with his inside shoulder, so that
he not only misses the correct line across the arena, but is also
crooked. The movement up the centre line, which is common to
all tests, is particularly crucial, since there is no arena perimeter to
act as a guide, and horse and rider are heading directly toward
the judge. To perform this movement well, it is essential that the
rider has an accurate picture of the line he wishes to take, and that
he keeps riding the horse actively forwards. The prior turn onto
the centre line is also very influential, and this will be discussed in
due course.
Circles and half-circles: In current preliminary level tests, all full
circles are of 20 metres diameter, but many of the half-circles (to
which the same technical criteria apply) are halves of 10 metre
circles.

A 20 metre circle from A or C must pass through X (the centre
point of the arena). It is especially important with these particular
circles that the rider concentrates upon correct shape; the first
and last quadrants of such circles pass across the corners of the
arena, and there is a tendency for both horse and rider to want to
go 'into' the corners, as if 'going large' round the arena. In the

context of a 20 metre circle, such a route is incorrect. A 20 metre circle started from a point on one long side of the arena must touch the other long side opposite the starting point (e.g. a 20 metre circle from E must pass through B).

A 10 metre half-circle started from a long side of the arena should touch, but not cross beyond, the centre line. Such figures demand accuracy and forethought, especially in cases where the line is not marked out (e.g. by a mown strip).

To ride a good circle, it is essential to begin at the right point and to establish the appropriate degree of correct bend. The first quarter of the circle is the most crucial because, if the rider gets this right, he has only to keep going to produce a good figure. If, however, the first quarter is poor, then the rider may spend the rest of the movement 'looking for' the circle. Where problems of shape *are* experienced, the rider must concentrate upon riding the horse 'out' or 'in' to the circle with his legs. Trying to influence the horse by leaning the upper body is a mistake – it will just unbalance him. The common tendency to try to 'hold the horse out' with the inside rein (by moving the inside hand across the wither) should be avoided, since the likely effects are to restrict movement and produce more inward bend of the neck. The most serious errors – already mentioned – are to attempt to correct the shape of the circle by direct uses of the reins alone.

In addition to assessing shape and location of circles, judges will be on the lookout for any changes – usually losses – of impulsion and rhythm. It should be remembered that it is physically harder for a horse to move on a circle than in a straight line, and the smaller the circle, the greater the degree of difficulty. There is, therefore, a natural tendency for horses to lose momentum on a circle, and the wise rider will prepare for this, asking for a little more energy just before starting the circle, supporting the horse with the aids throughout, and being constantly ready to counter any incipient loss of impulsion before it is actually obvious to the judge.

Half-circles do not appear in isolation; they normally form parts of movements which can be considered relatively complex at this level. Common examples are:

Two half-circles to change the rein: This figure is a good test for the rider's aid applications and the horse's responses, and it takes considerable concentration to perform well. The horse must describe half a circle from one long side of the arena to the centre line, followed immediately by a second half-circle on the other rein, thus moving in an 'S' shape across the arena. Smooth execution is facilitated if the horse is ridden straight for one stride on the centre line, thus giving the rider a moment to reverse the directional aids, and the horse a moment to respond. This straight stride will appear simply as a finishing of the first half-circle and start of the second, and will not be marked down. The rider should not, however, allow the horse to travel any significant distance down the centre line before starting the second half-circle, since this *would* be incorrect. (Since this movement can be performed either across the width of the arena – half 10 metre circles – or down its length – half 20 metre circles – the term 'centre line', in this instance, is used to describe either the actual centre line AC, or its equivalent EB.)

Half-circle followed by an incline: An incline is simply a straight line ridden to or from the outside track at an angle of other than 90 degrees. Thus the requirement for a half-circle followed by an incline might be 'FD half-circle right 10 metres diameter, returning to the track at B'. (D being the imaginary marker point on the centre line between K and F.) In order to ride such a figure smoothly (without an awkward join between the half-circle and the incline) it is necessary to perform slightly more than half a circle, and to think of the incline as a tangent from the circle.

Simple turns: Turns (i.e. 90 degree turns through corners) are performed simply by riding a quarter of a circle. According to B.H.S. Dressage Group rules, such turns at all working gaits should be ridden as a quarter of a circle of approximately 6 metres diameter. Desirable though this is, riders who have to cope with horses who are lacking in schooling and balance may make problems for themselves if attempting to stick slavishly to this rule at the faster gaits. In such circumstances, it makes sense to ride turns based upon the circles of sizes sufficient to enable the horse to retain impulsion, rhythm and balance. This does not mean, of course, that the rider of a less than perfectly schooled horse should automatically base all turns on 20 metre circles! Rather, a sensible compromise must be established, and this should be done in the practise arena, not on the spur of the moment when the test is in progress.

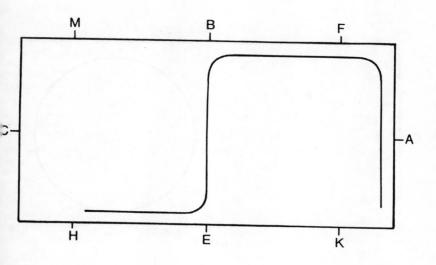

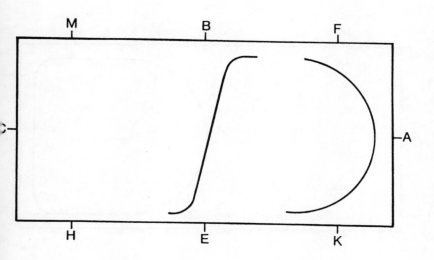

Examples of correct and incorrect figures
Turns across the arena in walk and trot *Top*: Correct *Bottom*: Incorrect

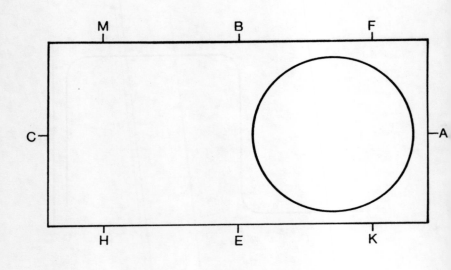

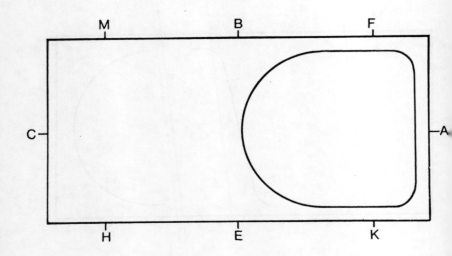

Examples of correct and incorrect figures
Riding a 20 metre circle *Top:* Correct *Bottom:* Incorrect

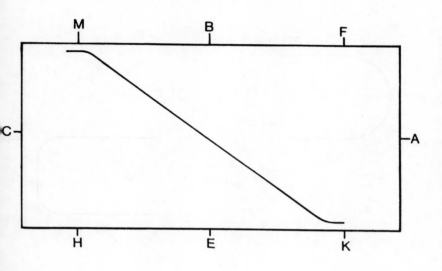

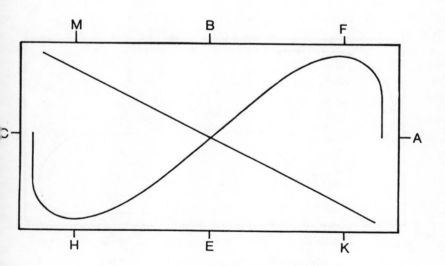

Examples of correct and incorrect figures
Riding across a long diagonal *Top:* Correct *Bottom* Incorrect

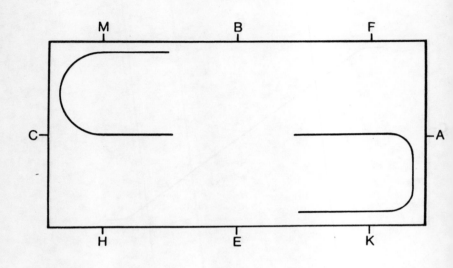

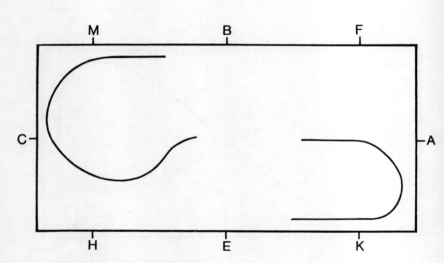

Examples of correct and incorrect figures
Top: Turning onto/from centre line *Left:* Via half a 10 metre circle *Right:* Strictly correct
Bottom: Incorrect turns onto/from centre line

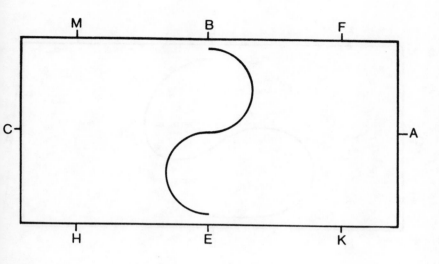

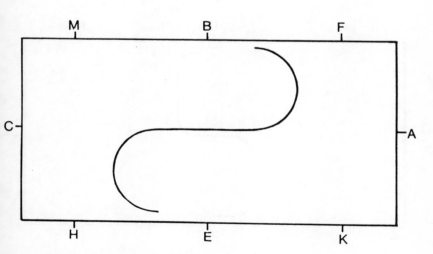

Examples of correct and incorrect figures
Top: Two half 10 metre circles to change the rein – correct
Bottom: Two half 10 metre circles to change the rein – incorrect – start and
finish points inaccurate – straight on centre line for too long

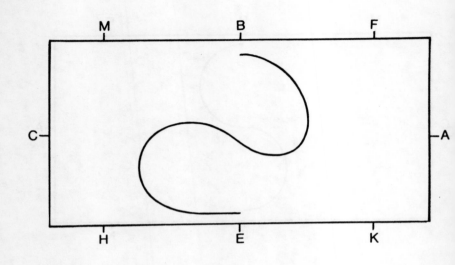

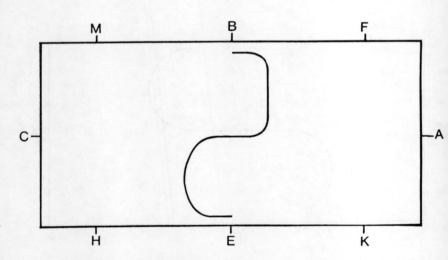

Examples of correct and incorrect figures
Top: Two half 10 metre circles to change the rein: incorrect – overlooping – shape inaccurate
Bottom: Two half 10 metre circles to change the rein – incorrect – too flat too shallow

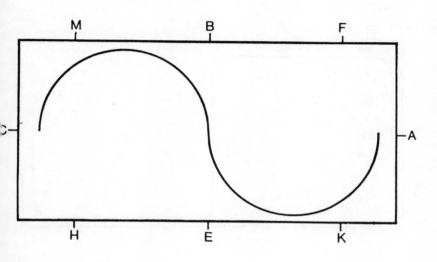

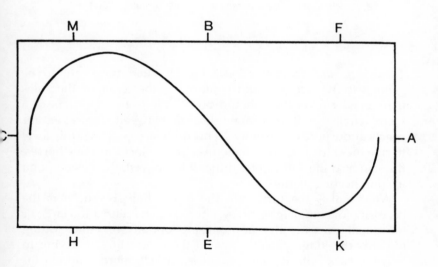

Examples of correct and incorrect figures
Top: Correct – *Bottom:* Incorrect. Two half 20 metre circles to change the rein

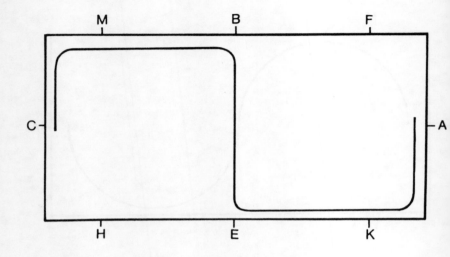

Examples of correct and incorrect figures
This figure is patently NOT two half 20 metre circles, but an extreme example of how the 'attraction' of the arena perimeter can destroy such a figure

Turns onto and from the centre line: If such turns are to be geometrically accurate, and conform to the letter of the rules mentioned above, they should be ridden as two quarters of 6 metre circles, with a straight line in between. However, for practical purposes, it usually seems quite acceptable at this level to ride these turns as half 10 metres circles. Since, on some horses, this can be quite sufficiently difficult to do well, there is no point in complicating matters.

What makes the turn onto the centre line so crucial is the necessity for complete accuracy; a turn which is either too large or too small presents the unpromising options of either riding towards the judge patently not on the centre line, or trying to 'wiggle' back onto it somehow. It is, in fact, more common for riders to overshoot this turn than to turn short, one reason being the tendency for many horses to anticipate that they will be moving across the short side of the arena rather than turning up

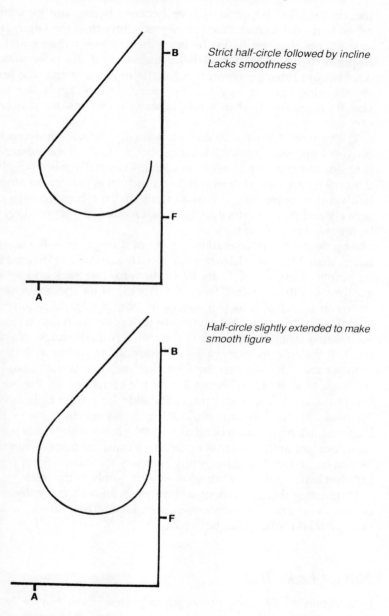

*Strict half-circle followed by incline
Lacks smoothness*

*Half-circle slightly extended to make
smooth figure*

Half-circle followed by incline

the centre. This happens simply because horses are generally asked to do the former much more frequently than the latter, and any anticipation results in the horse being slower than usual to respond to the aids. It may help, therefore, if the rider makes doubly sure during preparation for the movement that the hors is 'listening', and it may also be appropriate to apply the aids slightly more firmly than might otherwise be considered necessary.

The turn from the centre line is essentially the same movement, but it is a little easier since it is more obvious to the horse where he is to go, and the long side of the arena is normally more tangible than the centre line. However, when this turn is performed after a halt on the centre line, it is important that the horse moves off actively and straight, since an inactive, crooked gait is not likely to be followed by a good turn.

Shallow loop: This is essentially an arc of a large circle (i.e. much larger than 20 metres diameter). A specific loop will be defined by its points of departure from, and return to, the track and by its greatest depth (distance from the track). Thus the movement 'between F and M a loop 5 metres in from the track' requires a symmetrical figure whose mid-point (opposite the B marker) is 5 metres (a quarter of the width of the arena) from the track. We can use this specific movement as an example of riding a shallow loop: as the rider reaches the F marker, he directs the horse off the track as if about to incline across the arena but, as the horse leaves the track, the rider applies the aids for a little right bend. He must, at this juncture, be looking at the centre point of the loop and asking for such bend as will take him through this point on a constant arc. This arc is maintained until the horse nears the M marker, when the rider gently reverses the aids, asking for a little left bend so that the horse returns smoothly to the track.

Performing this movement well requires smooth co-ordination of the aids, and the previously discussed errors made when riding circles must, again, be avoided.

Novice Level Tests

In addition to the movements already described, novice level tests require the following:

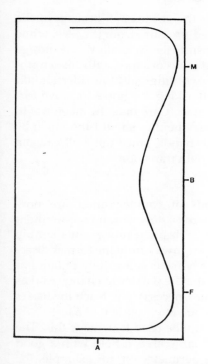

Five metre loop from F to M.

GAIT VARIANTS *Lengthened strides at trot and canter:* It should be noted that the requirement is only for 'lengthened strides', and not specifically for medium or extended gaits – although either of these would fit the bill. The object at this level is simply to show that the horse can increase stride length somewhat from the working gaits, and there is no need for the rider to be over-ambitious.

It *is* important, however, that the horse lengthens correctly. He should retain the same stride frequency (number of strides per given period) as in the working gait, but travel faster by virtue of the strides being longer. 'Running' – travelling faster by taking short, quick strides – has nothing to do with correct lengthening; it merely constitutes poor gait quality.

Lengthened strides are required across a long diagonal or down a long side of the arena. Since the number of strides is not specified, the wise rider will seek to produce sufficient to satisfy the judge, while allowing himself enough room before and after to make smooth transitions from and to working gait.

65

The basic aids for lengthening the strides are: bracing of the back in conjunction with increased pressure from the legs, while the hands soften the rein contact sufficiently to allow/encourage the horse to lengthen his outline in accordance with his lengthened strides. To re-establish the working gait, the rider should soften the driving aids while still asking the horse to move forward into a more 'containing' contact. Care must be taken not to pull on the reins (always an error), neither should the horse be driven too vigorously into 'hard' hands, since this will cause a break in rhythm rather than a smooth transition.

COUNTER-CANTER Brief periods of counter-canter are now required in some novice tests. There is, however, no requirement to counter-canter circles or part circles; the movements simply require a few strides of 'dog-legging' away from the former direction of travel. Nevertheless, if the horse is completely unfamiliar with counter-canter it is possible that he will try to change lead as he changes direction. It is, therefore, necessary to teach the basics of counter-canter at home well before attempting it in a test.

There are two exercises which can be used to achieve this. The first is best performed in a fairly large area; a field with a good surface is ideal. Trot around the perimeter on, for example, the right rein then, on a long, straight line ask for *left* canter. With the canter established, sit very still and quietly maintain the aids for left lead, especially a slight flexion to the left rein. Look a little to the right, open the right rein a little and ask the horse to move on a gentle curve to the right. When he has responded for a few strides without resisting or trying to change legs, straighten him and ride forwards. Do not be too demanding at first; a few strides on a slight curve will suffice. When this has been achieved, a few more strides *or* a slightly greater curve can be requested, but the horse must be straightened *before* he begins to struggle or resist.

The second exercise can be performed once the first has proved successful. Proceed around the arena in, for example, left canter, ensuring a good working gait. Starting down a long side, just before the first quarter marker, take the horse off the track at a *slight* angle so that, when level with B or E, he will be only a couple of metres in from the outside track. Upon nearing B or E, maintain the aids for left lead but, as previously, ask the horse to curve to the right, so as

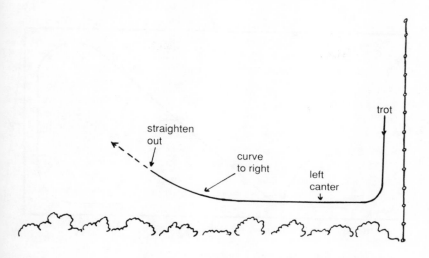

Exercise 1

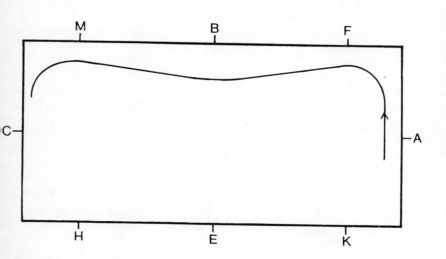

Exercise 2

Exercises in maintaining lead while introducing opposite bend (to be performed on both reins)

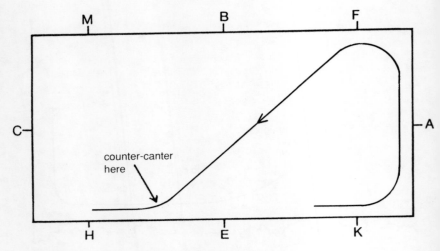

Typical set up for counter-canter in novice tests

to rejoin the outside track before the next quarter marker. Upon reaching the track, relinquish the aids to move right and straighten the horse before going through the corner in correct bend.

Both exercises must be practised on each rein, using patience to achieve success. Once they can be performed consistently and correctly, there should be no real difficulty with the movements of the novice tests. (Although a rider competing in such tests on a hired horse will be largely at the mercy of the horse's prior training he can, whilst riding-in, at least attempt these exercises to discover the horse's aptitude.)

FIGURES *15 metre circle:* Although a half 15 metre circle is featured in one of the older preliminary tests, the 15 metre circle does not appear in current tests until novice level. Technically, it presents no special problems, but its correct size is perhaps harder to visualise than that of the 10 and 20 metre figures. Ridden from a point on a long side, its diameter will be three-quarters of the width of the arena, and it is as well to have this firmly in mind before starting the figure.

Serpentines: A serpentine is a consecutive series of arcs, half-circles or loops of equal size, curving in alternate directions (thus the two half 10 metre circles to change the rein is a simple serpentine). In cases where the total width of the figure required is greater than the diameter of the half-circles upon which it is based, there will be short straight sections between the curves, which make such a figure easier to ride than one consisting entirely of constantly changing loops. Both the serpentines required in novice level tests contain straight sections, and problems are more likely to concern accuracy rather than technique.

The most common inaccuracies are failure to produce loops of equal size, and irregularities of shape. These can be overcome by giving prior consideration to the geometry of the figure, and by ensuring that the first loop is ridden correctly (one incorrect loop automatically and irrevocably affecting the rest of the serpentine).

The serpentines ridden at novice level are:

1) Three loops from A, covering whole arena and finishing at C. This is probably the most commonly-ridden serpentine. In the short arena, it consists of three half-circles of approximately 13 metres diameter, with a couple of strides of straight lines between each. The main difficulty lies in trying to visualise the arena divided into thirds, since there are no markers which can readily be used as guidelines. The only one which is of any practical use is the mid-point marker on the long side, which marks the mid-point of this serpentine, and should thus be passed halfway through the second loop.

2) Two loops between C and X, each going to the side of the arena. The fact that this is ridden within the confines of a 20 metre square, and its construction – two half 10 metre circles interspersing three straight lines – make it relatively easy to visualise and ride. The rider proceeds straight three-quarters of the way across the short side of the arena, then rides a half-circle to a line midway between the short side and the EXB line. He proceeds three-quarters of the way across the arena, and rides the second half-circle in the other direction, finishing on the EXB line. Care should be taken not to ride right into the corner of the arena when starting the first half-circle but, providing this is ridden accurately, the rest of the figure should fall into place.

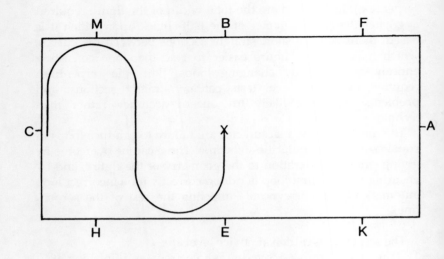

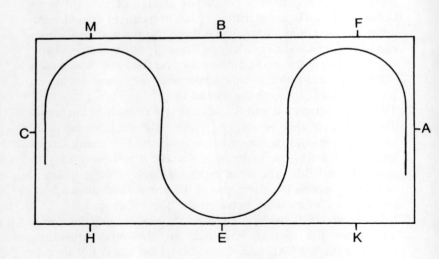

Top: CX serpentine two loops, each loop going to the side of the arena
Bottom: Correct three-loop serpentine over whole arena

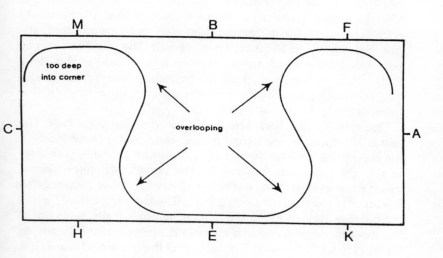

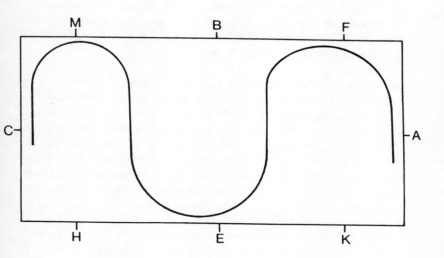

Top: Incorrect three-loop serpentine
Bottom: Incorrect. Unequal loops.

REIN-BACK The requirements of a good rein-back are that it is straight, with regular steps and no resistance from the horse. As with other movements, preparation is of great importance, the pre-requisite being a square, attentive halt. The rein-back will be performed from the centre marker on a short side of the arena and, to achieve the square halt, the preceding corner must be ridden accurately, so that the horse is moving on a straight line immediately prior to halting.

The aids for rein-back are an extension of those for halt. The halt is produced in the usual manner but, once it is established, the rider does not ease the aids, but continues to use leg pressure to ride the horse into still hands. The horse is, therefore, being asked for movement, but not being allowed to move forwards, so he can only respond by moving back. The most important factors in applying the aids are to apply them symmetrically, so as not to induce crookedness, and to remember the principle of riding from the hindquarters forward. Trying to pull the horse backwards is a grave error, which will produce resistances and destroy the regularity of the steps.

Immediately the rein-back is completed, the test requires the horse to go forward in medium walk. To make the transition, upon completing the rein-back, the rider momentarily eases all aids, then re-applies his legs, keeping the rein contact light and thus allowing the horse forward.

RELEASING AND REGAINING THE REIN CONTACT At novice level, there were originally two ways – other than free walk on a long rein – in which the rider was required to release and regain and rein contact; by 'stroking the horse's neck' (performed at working canter) and by 'giving and retaking the reins' (performed at working canter and working trot). There have been various intentions behind these movements, and various interpretations of them. Current rules refer only to 'give and retake the reins', but 'stroke the horse's neck' still appears as an instruction in Novice 17.

'Stroking the horse's neck' does not mean doing so in a normally recognised sense; the requirement is for the rider to push both hands up the horse's neck until rein contact is surrendered, and then to retake the contact. The purpose is to demonstrate that the horse is achieving self- carriage (is balanced, and not 'leaning' on the rider's hands). Initially, the intention was that the rider's hands should remain forwards for a short while, but it was subsequently considered that the degree of engagement of the horse's hind limbs necessary for success in the movement was over-demanding at this level. 'Stroking the neck' may now, therefore, be performed in one continuous forward and back motion.

The principle, however, remains the same, and success or failure will be largely dependent upon the horse's level of training. Nevertheless, the rider will certainly help his cause by remembering to keep riding the horse 'forwards'; engagement of the hocks remains the key to success, and deficiency in this department will almost certainly result in the horse running/falling onto his forehand. Also, the rider should avoid the temptation to hurry the movement by 'throwing' the reins at the horse and snatching them back, since this will only disturb his equilibrium.

'Giving and retaking the reins' was originally envisaged as having the dual purpose of showing that the horse was learning to move correctly, and was prepared to accept changes in rein contact without evasions or changes of rhythm.

The first part of the requirement, 'giving' the reins, is used extensively at the end of training sessions, when the horse is allowed, by mouthing the bit, to gradually take the reins through the rider's fingers, the intention being that he takes the contact gently forwards and down by stretching his neck in that direction. This both rewards the horse, and demonstrates to the rider that his work has been along the right lines. In such a context, the exercise is most valuable, and it may be demonstarted at the end of any dressage test, where the instruction is to 'leave the arena at free walk on a long rein'. Unfortunately, in the context in which it was incorporated into the movement 'give and retake the reins', it was of little use, because the timescale was too short. Furthermore, the movement as a whole gave rise to confusion among both competitors and judges, and it has now been decided that it should be performed in one continuous movement, effectively that of 'stroking the horse's neck' in the new manner defined above.

6

Rules for Dressage Tests

The question of familiarity with rules for dressage competitions is one which can be easily ignored or overlooked by those who think it is just a case of performing the test and being marked for it. However, although the rules for dressage are somewhat less elaborate than those for jumping competitions, there is more to them than may be apparent, and it is important to be aware of them in order to avoid disappointment resulting from neglect of a technicality. At the highest level, the rules for dressage are laid down by the F.E.I. (Fédération Equestre Internationale) the body governing international equestrian sport, and the rules of the British Horse Society Dressage Group (*Dressage Rules and Official Judges Panel*) are very closely based upon the F.E.I. rules. In turn, the *Rules For Official Competitions* produced by the Riding Club Committee of the British Horse Society are essentially those of the Dressage Group, slightly tailored to suit the circumstances of Riding Club members. The Pony Club rules are also based on the Dressage Group rules, but differ significantly with regard to tack permitted for certain tests.

The Dressage Group rules are constant for all competitions of a given level, but those of the Riding and Pony Clubs may vary slightly depending upon which specific competition is being held. A further complication, pertaining to all three sets of rules, is the distinction between 'pure' dressage, and the dressage phase of horse trials. It is, therefore, in the competitor's interest to ascertain exactly which rules will apply to any given competition. In the case of competitions affiliated to the B.H.S. Dressage Group, the matter will be cut and dry, but it should be borne in mind that *all* the relevant rules will apply to *all* competitions, and attention to detail is the order of the day. Some unaffiliated competitions may also be run under Dressage Group rules, but this should be apparent from the schedule/entry form.

In most events organised by riding clubs, the general rules for riding club competitions will apply, the more specific rules for area competitions and championships being applied at those events. At some less formal club shows, it is possible that certain rules may be waived, although this can cause confusion if the organisers neglect to inform the judge of their intentions! Many judges, even at minor events, are on the official B.H.S. panel and/ or compete themselves at formal level, and will automatically apply the rules as they know them, unless otherwise requested.

At competitions organised by the Pony Club for members only, it is virtually certain that their own rules will be in force. However, Pony Club branches not infrequently hold 'open' competitions, and these may be run under Dressage Group rules. In the absence of information on the schedule, this matter is well worth checking.

Since the various rules are readily available, it would serve no purpose to reproduce them in detail, but it may be worth looking at some of those which are of common relevance, in order to emphasise the need to pay them due attention. The following are paraphrased extracts from the B.H.S. Dressage Group rules (applicable to preliminary and novice levels), with variations in Riding Club and Pony Club rules noted as appropriate. (It should be borne in mind that rules from all these bodies are subject to minor annual alterations).

Rules Relating to the Physical Condition of the Horse

AGE   The minimum age at which a horse may compete at dressage is four years.

HEIGHT   There are no height restrictions.

EQUINE INFLUENZA VACCINATIONS   All horses registered with the B.H.S. Dressage Group must be vaccinated as directed under their rules. Vaccination certificates must be taken to all B.H.S.D.G. competitions. Spot checks are carried out at which the certificate must be produced: failure to do so resulting in elimination. Under Riding Club rules, vaccination it is a condition of participation in official competitions. There is no stipulation in the Pony Club rules.

At most local shows, there is no requirement to produce a certificate, or even for the horse to be vaccinated. However, where a competition is held on land belonging to a breeding or racing establishment, it is highly likely that the organisers will insist upon a certificate as a condition of entry.

FORBIDDEN SUBSTANCES These are defined as 'any stimulant, sedative or substance other than a normal nutrient'. (Given the ingredients in some commercially-produced horse feeds, one is tempted to question what constitutes a 'normal' nutrient.) If such a substance is discovered by a random test, its presence will normally result in elimination, the exception being that levels of Phenylbutazone or Oxyphenbutazone ('bute') below 2 micrograms per millilitre of plasma are permitted. If it is necessary to treat a horse with a drug during the course of competition, the vet responsible to the organisers must be informed, and, in the light of his opinion, the organisers will decide whether the horse shall be permitted to continue participating.

LAMENESS In the case of marked lameness, the horse will be eliminated from the competition. If there is some doubt about soundness, the competitor may be allowed to complete the test, but any unevenness of movement will be penalised in the marking. Even if the test is completed, the judge may seek veterinary opinion before allowing the competitor's score to stand – that is to say that the horse may be effectively eliminated even after completing the test – a fact which can have considerable impact on a team event.

Rules Relating to the Physical Condition of the Rider

DISABLED RIDERS A rider whose physical disability prevents his riding in accordance with the standard rules may apply to the B.H.S. Dressage Group for a special dispensation certificate, which must be shown to the judge before riding the test. The Riding Club rules make reference to a dispensation regarding the use of adapted reins; in other cases advice is that organisers should be notified at the time of entry. The Riding For The Disabled Association now holds various equestrian competitions, and their own rules can be obtained direct.

FORBIDDEN SUBSTANCES Dressage Group rules list a large number of forbidden substances, many of which may be present in bona fida medications. Riders participating in 'serious' competitions while taking prescribed drugs would be advised to consult their doctor on this matter, otherwise they may risk failing a 'dope test.'

CONCUSSION Pony Club rules prohibit a rider who has suffered concussion from riding again on the same day under any circumstances, and on subsequent days until passed fit by a doctor.

Rules Relating to the Rider's Dress and Equipment

GENERAL CLOTHING Dressage Group rules permit uniform and what is effectively hunt dress or hacking jacket with bowler hat, hunt cap or crash cap, and specify that, unless they form part of a uniform, breeches must be white, cream or beige. It is obligatory to wear gloves.

Riding Club rules refer to 'correct riding clothes', and specify the wearing of a hat conforming to BS 6473 or BS 4472.

Pony Club rules specify a tweed, navy or black coat, with a white stock or Pony Club tie, and specify that 'dark-coloured breeches may not be worn'. They insist upon the wearing of a hat to BS 4472 (the 'crash hat' or 'jockey skull'), and this must be complete with chin harness and a dark blue or black cover. Under Pony Club rules, if a hat comes off during the test, or the chinstrap becomes undone, the competitor must replace/refasten it before continuing, the penalty for non-compliance being elimination. Although there is no additional penalty for dismounting to retrieve the hat, or having it passed up, no marks are awarded for the movement during which it came off.

SPURS May be worn at all levels of competition under Dressage Group rules (interestingly, they are *compulsory* for tests of medium standard and above). There are, however, restrictions upon type, which are detailed in the rule books. Both Riding Club and Pony Club rules permit spurs but, again, subject to similar constraints regarding design and potential severity. In general terms, short, blunt spurs of standard design are permitted under all rules.

WHIP   A whip of any length may be carried, but, if it is dropped during the test, it may not be retrieved. There is no requirement to carry the whip in a particular hand, except that it should be in the rein hand when saluting (so that the rider does not poke himself or his horse in the eye). Misuse of the whip will result in elimination, but this does not mean that it cannot be used properly if the rider considers it necessary to do so.

The exception to this rule is that Riding Club rules do not permit a whip to be carried at the R.C. Championship (except, under special dispensation, by a disabled rider, or any competitor riding side-saddle), or in any tests forming part of horse trials, and the B.H.S. *Horse Trials* Committee rules also prohibit a whip during the dressage phase. Most local horse trials apply this 'no whip during dressage' rule, but it should be noted that in *dressage with* (*show*) *jumping* competitions, the Dressage Group rules – which permit a whip – usually apply.

JEWELLERY   Riding Club rules prohibit the wearing of earrings, ear or nose studs, and other items of jewellery which could cause injury or discomfort if caught or tangled. The Pony Club prohibit the wearing of earrings, on penalty of elimination.

Rules Relating to Tack, Saddlery and Equipment of the Horse

BITS AND BRIDLES   At preliminary and novice level, only snaffles are permitted (detailed definitions of 'snaffles' may be found in the rule book). The noseband must be a drop, flash or cavesson; grakles are permitted only if the test forms part of a horse trial. The Pony Club rules are basically the same for the main current tests, and Part 1 of their rule book suggests that a snaffle must be used for all of their dressage tests. However, Part 3 makes it apparent that some of their junior tests continue to permit the use of a double bridle, pelham or, in some cases, 'other'. Also, the test sheets for the 'D' and 'C' level tests stipulate that these can be ridden in 'any normal riding bit'. A pelham, where permitted, must be used with two sets of reins, or single reins attached to roundings.

Under all rules, martingales, bearing, side or running reins are prohibited, although it is permissible to lunge in side reins before the test. Bit guards are no longer allowed.

SADDLERY Saddles must be of English or Continental type. Dressage Group rules stipulate that the saddle must be brown, black, grey or navy, and the Pony Club rules permit only brown or black, used with a white or dark-coloured girth.

Breastplates are allowed. Dressage Group and Riding Club rules permit a neckstrap while riding-in and in preliminary level tests, but the Pony Club permit this item for riding-in only.

OTHER EQUIPMENT Brushing or over-reach boots and banda-ges may be used when working in, but are not permitted during the test, although substitutes for conventional shoes (Equiboots) are allowed.

Blinkers and hoods are prohibited. Fly-repellent browbands or discs are allowed during the test, but other protection from flies (fringes, gauzes, ear covers etc.) are only allowed for riding-in.

Regarding dress, tack and equipment; a steward should be on hand to check that all is in order, but the final responsibility rests with the competitor. Thus, if the steward is not available, does not know the rules, or just misses something, the rider may still be penalised for any contravention.

Rules Relating to the Performance of the Test

TIME The approximate time for performing the test shown on some tests sheets is purely for information; there is no time penalty system in force. The other time issue which should be borne in mind concerns the desirability of reporting to the appropriate steward a few minutes before one's allotted test time (even if a competition is known to be running late). At most dressage competitions, or competitions of which dressage forms a phase, competitors will be liable to elimination if they do not present themselves within a certain period of their allotted times.

ENTERING THE ARENA No horse (ridden or led) may enter the competition arena except when actually competing, on penalty of elimination. However, this ruling seems to be aimed at prevent-ing illicit practising (e.g. to familiarise the horse with a new arena surface, unfamiliar arena markings, etc.), since the rules go on to say that a rider entering the arena/starting the test before receiving the judge's signal *may* be eliminated.

In some cases – for instance, most indoor schools, – it is impossible for the competitor to ride around the outside of the arena whilst awaiting permission to start. In such circumstances, it is permissible to enter the arena and ride around the perimeter once the judge/organiser has invited one to do so.

EXECUTION OF THE TEST   *Order of movements*. All movements must be ridden in the prescribed order, and no extraneous movements are permitted, unless the judge indicates an error of course and directs the rider to return to a certain point and restart a movement. In any other case where a competitor attempts to re-ride a movement, the judge will mark only that part of the movement first performed and will also penalise the rider for an error of course.

Errors of course. Basically, an error of course is when a rider departs from the direction/figure/gait laid down in the test (although it is not adjudged an error of course if the rider is trying to perform a certain gait, but is unable to elicit it from the horse). If an error of course is made, the judge will sound his signal to indicate the error and halt the competitor, and will point out, if necessary, where and how to resume the test. The penalties for errors of course are the loss of two marks for the first error, a further four marks for the second error, a further eight marks for the third, and elimination thereafter.

Errors of test. The phrase 'error of test' does not refer to riding the wrong test (for which the penalty is elimination), but to details such as saluting incorrectly, or starting/finishing a movement at the wrong marker through rider error. It is not normally necessary for the judge to interrupt the test on such occasions, but the error will be noted on the mark sheet, and each error will be penalised by the loss of two marks.

Reins. The test should be ridden with the reins in both hands, the exception being when saluting the judge (some tests at higher levels also specify that certain movements be ridden with the reins in one hand). However, if a rider needs to use a whip, and removes his whip hand from the rein, it is unlikely that this would be considered an infringement.

Trot work. Although some of the older tests specify that certain movements be ridden in sitting or rising trot, this ruling no longer applies (except in Prix Caprilli tests). Under Dressage Group rules, at these levels, the rider has the option to sit or rise, and this also applies under Riding Club and Pony Club rules.

Dismounting and falling. If, whilst in the arena, a competitor dismounts without a reason acceptable to the judge, no marks will be awarded for the movement concerned. In the event of a fall, the competitor will be penalised only by the effect of the fall on the marks for the movement in which it occurred, although perceived reasons for the fall may be taken into account when the judge awards collective marks at the end of the test.

Resistance. This term is used to describe a horse refusing to move forwards – obviously a serious fault at any time. Under Dressage Group rules, a horse failing to enter the arena within 60 seconds of the signal being sounded will be eliminated. If, during the test, a horse 'resists' for 20 consecutive seconds he, also, will be eliminated. Under Riding Club and Pony Club rules, the same penalty applies for refusal to enter the arena, but the period of resistance allowed during the test is extended to 60 consecutive seconds.

It should be noted that grinding the teeth and swishing the tail are considered *signs* of resistance in the horse (and will result in his being marked down) but they do not, of themselves, constitute 'full scale' resistance as described above.

Voice. Despite the fact that all the equestrian text books will tell you that the voice is a natural aid, its use during a dressage test is not permitted, and each use will be penalised by the deduction of two marks.

Leaving the arena. At the end of all tests the horse should leave the arena at a free walk on a long rein at the A marker, this movement forming the final part of the test. Leaving the arena involuntarily during the test is penalised in the following ways:

1) If there is a continuous surround to the arena (usually white boards) 9 inches (22cm) or more in height, and the horse leaves the arena, he is eliminated.

2) If there is a continuous surround less than 9 inches (22cm) in height, no marks will be awarded for any movement during which the horse places all four feet outside the arena.

3) If the surround has no height (e.g. consists of painted lines), or the markers are intermittent, marks will be awarded at the

judge's discretion. A horse leaving the arena 'not under control' will be eliminated.

COMMANDED TESTS Whilst it is normal practice to ride dressage tests from memory, it is sometimes permissible to have them 'commanded'. This entails having someone call out the movements of the test as it is being ridden, so that a competitor can perform the test without having first learnt it. Commanding is allowed in most competitions (except area level, finals and championships) under Dressage Group, Riding Club and Pony Club rules, but not normally in the dressage phase of a horse trial run under the B.H.S. Horse Trials Committee or any other organising body's rules. If a competitor wishes to have a test commanded, it is wise to check with the organisers first, and it is a matter of courtesy to inform the judge beforehand.

The rules covering commanded tests are quite strict; the commander must only call out the movements laid down; any advice or assistance – even involuntary and unsolicited – will result in the competitor's elimination. Furthermore, the effectiveness and accuracy of the commands, and the interpretation of them, are deemed to be the competitor's responsibility; no allowance is made for incorrect, inaudible or misconstrued commands. Regarding audibility, it should be noted that a commander should be positioned near E or B (to avoid obscuring the judge's view), and it makes sense to choose the siting where any wind will be at the commander's back.

Commanding well is really quite difficult, especially with regard to timing, and it is essential that the person doing it is intimately familiar with the test – and preferably a rider themselves. Even if a test is commanded skilfully, the rider can only respond to the commands, and will have little time to think ahead and prepare for changes of gait, direction, etc.

There are times when having a test commanded may be either necessary (for instance, if a rider is called upon to act as a last-minute team substitute) or useful (if there are other, more important, tests to remember, and the commanded test is being used as a 'school'). However, it is probable that any rider would always perform a test he had learnt properly better than the same test commanded, and this brings us to the question of the learning process.

7

Learning a Test

Interpreting the Test Sheet

In order to learn a test correctly, it is first necessary to understand fully the requirements laid down on the test sheet. Newcomers to dressage sometimes find this off-putting at first glance, but anyone familiar with arena layout and the required figures and gaits will soon realise that a test is not as complicated as it may initially appear on paper. Since we have already dealt with these issues, we need now concern ourselves only with accurate interpretation of the demands of the test.

There are two main points which may require clarification. Firstly, the numbering of movements is primarily to facilitate judging. While it is essential for the judge to know where each designated movement starts and finishes, it is of no great importance to the rider, who will benefit more from visualising the test as a smooth, flowing whole, rather than a series of separate movements. Certainly, he must become intimately familiar with the *sequence* of the test, but there is little value in making a conscious effort to memorise it in terms of 'movement one, do this, movement two, do that', especially since it is not unusual for consecutive movements to be performed in the same gait.

Secondly, the test is described in a series of very brief instructions. This is desirable, since it avoids distracting clutter, but there are occasions when the instructions assume some understanding of the compiler's precise intentions. The most prevalent example of this is the assumption (confirmed in the rule book, but not on the test sheet) that, in the absence of specific instruction to the contrary, the rider will continue around the outside track in the last prescribed gait and direction.

This matter is not quite as straightforward as it may sound; consider, for example, the instruction 'BE, working trot'. In the light of the above, it will be apparent that the requirement is to proceed around the outside track from B to E. However, in the absence of such knowledge, a rider could hardly be derided for riding a 90 degree turn at B and trotting straight across the arena or even, conceivably, trotting half a 20 metre circle between the two markers. Over the years, stranger interpretations than these examples have been observed, and it pays to make close examination of the test instructions in context, and to *ensure* that they are correctly understood from the beginning.

With reference to the alternative examples above, actual test instructions would be written thus:

To turn across arena – 'At B, turn left, at E, track left (or right)'. Note that 'turn', unqualified, always means a 90 degree turn. 'Track' means 'turn' onto the outside track.

For a half-circle – 'At (from) B, half-circle left, 20 metres diameter'. Note that this, and the ensuing instruction, may well *assume* that the half-circle will be completed at E; for instance, the next instruction might be 'between K and A, working canter left'.)

Committing the Test to Memory

This is a crucial part in the whole process of riding dressage tests. A competitor who has fully memorised the test, to the point where recall is automatic, can concentrate exclusively upon riding, while a competitor whose knowledge of the test is somewhat sketchy will be preoccupied with trying to remember what to do next; a state of affairs which can prove detrimental not only to his riding technique, but also to smooth presentation of the test.

It is a fact that some quite experienced riders retain a disproportionate (and usually unjustified) dread of losing their way. This is usually a form of 'pre-match nerves', which evaporates once they enter the arena and, if it increases their determination to learn the test thoroughly, it may be no bad thing. However, if this can happen to the experienced, it is not surprising that many less experienced competitors will be similarly affected, the difference being that their very inexperience can result in their taking their fears into the arena so that, regardless of how well they know the

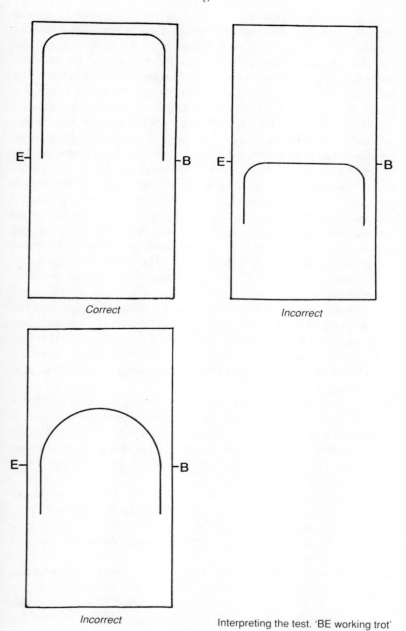

Correct

Incorrect

Incorrect

Interpreting the test. 'BE working trot'

test, they concentrate upon route rather than riding. This is actually quite natural, and can be explained by the rider's relative familiarity with the technical demands of the movements compared to his unfamiliarity with actually performing the test as a whole (for instance, he is pretty certain he will be able to canter, but less certain that he will remember where to do so). While it is likely that such an approach will result in the competitor actually riding a little below his capabilities, it should at least ensure that he does *not* lose his way, and, once a few tests have been completed without error, he will grow in confidence, to the benefit of his subsequent performances. In order to reach this stage however, the newcomer must not baulk at the initial prospect of learning the test, and be tempted into having it commanded. Precisely how a test is learnt is very much a matter for the individual. Everyone has their own preferred learning processes, and those of dressage competitors vary between the painstaking, the blasé and the bizarre. The following points are, therefore, offered simply as guidelines based upon personal experience:

1) In the early stages, it makes sense to attempt just one test per competition, so that full attention can be given to learning and riding it as well as possible. The only exception is when it is possible to ride the same test in two different classes, in which case the rider may wish to have two attempts at the test, and compare marks.

2) With practise an experienced rider can, if necessary, learn a basic level test in ten or fifteen minutes. However, such haste is never desirable, and would be impractical for an inexperienced rider. If circumstances permit, it is best to start learning the test several days before the competition, spending a few quiet minutes at a time on it.

3) First of all, read through the test several times. Concentrate upon retaining a mental picture of the route, and note prescribed gaits and gait variants, and the location of transitions. Do not, however, make a conscious effort to commit the whole test to memory in one go.

4) After several such readings, sketch out an arena, and try to run through the test with a pencil, using perhaps a dotted line for walk, dashes for trot and solid line for canter. Gait variants can be indicated by altered lines – for instance, longer dashes for

lengthened strides at trot. If *at all* unsure of the next movement, refer back to the test sheet; do not guess – you don't
want to learn the test incorrectly. Initially, such runs-through
should all be thoroughly checked, but, after a little practise,
you should find that you can reproduce the test readily and
accurately.

5) At this juncture, start trying to visualise actually riding the
test. Imagine an arena, and imagine riding the movements,
allotting a realistic timescale to each. This will really help to
imprint the test upon the memory, and will assist in bringing
to your attention the need for preparation, and other practical
concerns. If you will not be able to practise the test on
horseback prior to the competition, this exercise becomes
invaluable.

Mounted Practise

Running through the test on horseback is the next logical step but,
in the first instance, this should be done with the emphasis on
consolidating the rider's knowledge of the test. Therefore,
although you should ride as well as possible, you should not
worry too much about the niceties at first. If, for instance, a
movement is performed poorly, do not interrupt the test for a re-
ride; continue it as laid down. Practising without second chances
will not only be more useful as far as the basic learning process is
concerned, it can also highlight potential difficulties in the test,
and you can concentrate upon these, and general techniques, in
due course.

Runs-through of this nature can be useful even if you are not on
the horse you are to ride in the test itself, although it is important
that the 'practise' horse is capable of performing the movements
to a reasonable standard, or else you may become side-tracked
into a schooling session, and generally distracted from the object
of the exercise.

It may seem somewhat paradoxical to suggest that, if you *are*
able to practise on the horse you will ride in the test, you should
be sparing in the number of complete runs-through you perform.
However, on the one hand there is the risk of both horse and rider
becoming stale, and on the other hand there is the risk of the rider
becoming blasé, and the horse starting to anticipate. While the

drawbacks of staleness and indifference are obvious, anticipation must be avoided since it can result in hurried or premature transitions, or even in the horse attempting to change gait at a moment when no change is called for.

In order to reduce the risk of such problems, a suggested programme for a practise session would be a few minutes general warm-up, a period of more concentrated work to gain the horse's full attention (transitions, half-halts, figure work and perhaps a little leg-yielding), and then a test run-through. In the event of the result being highly satisfactory, it may be best to call it a day at this juncture but, assuming that there will some areas which need attention, the horse should be given a short period of relaxation (free walk on a long rein) while the rider marshals his thoughts, and some time should then be spent on problem movements (although they should not be practised repeatedly in the same place). Once some improvement is apparent, another run-through should be made, and then, for better or worse, the session should be brought to a close with some straightforward winding down exercises.

It is important not to fall into the trap of following such a pattern every day for several days before a test, otherwise the problems associated with repetition may still occur. It is better to alternate practise days with different activities, such as jumping or hacking. If there is any aspect of the test which is proving especially problematical, this can be worked on for a short session before riding out, but it will prove more fruitful if such sessions are not undertaken at times when the rider is tired, confused or desperate and it may, of course, be a great help to work on the problem under instruction.

8

The Judge's Viewpoint

If we assume that the competitor will be seeking to obtain the best possible mark for a test, it becomes important to have some prior understanding of how the judge is likely to assess what he sees. This may seem obvious, and it is easy to say 'he will want to see a good test', but things are not quite that straightforward; it is necessary to know both what criteria are being applied and, as far as possible, what emphasis the judge is likely to place upon various factors.

The judge's brief is basically to see how the principles of correct equitation are applied to the movements of the test, and to assess each movement with a mark of between 0 and 10. There are also collective marks to be awarded at the end of the test for overall impression of various factors; impulsion, submission, seat and aids of rider, etc. Thus the judge's task is, in theory, quite straightforward – it is when he tries to carry it out consistently, fairly and accurately that the practical difficulties come into play.

Whereas an instructor can spend some time assessing horse and rider in individual gaits and figures, the judge must start to assess a (probably unfamiliar) horse immediately he enters the arena, and to mark movements which may each contain several different elements, performed with varying degrees of proficiency. Furthermore, since the individual movements vary so much in content – and because of timescale, and the need to produce comments as well as marks – the judge has neither the logical basis nor the time to be mathematically analytical; that is to say, he cannot make a prior decision to give up to x marks a movement for impulsion, y marks for bend, or whatever. He must, therefore, draw upon his experience to award marks on a basis of general impression and 'gut feeling', seasoned with his immediate assessment of particularly good or bad moments.

Although a good judge can perform this task most effectively, it would be asking too much of anyone to start judging a competition completely devoid of pre-conceived ideas or 'bench marks' upon which to base their assessments. Thus judges invariably start out with a broadly-based mental order of merit of the things they would like to see, and a similar list of dislikes, or even pet hates. It is acknowledging these factors that gives the rider the best chance of maximising his marks.

Obviously, judges being human, their individual likes and dislikes will vary to some degree, as will their overall assessment of the good, bad and indifferent elements which make up the vast majority of dressage tests. It would, therefore, be unrealistic to attempt a detailed relative listing of 'do's' and 'don'ts', or to claim that such a listing would be universally applicable. However, since judges (should) share a deep knowledge of equitation, it is not surprising that they usually place most emphasis upon the presence or absence of the same key factors, especially impulsion and accuracy.

At preliminary and novice level, reasonable judges will be conscious of the fact that they are looking at horses at a relatively early stage of training or, perhaps, at school horses who are normally ridden by a number of people of varying degrees of proficiency. They will not, therefore, expect perfection, but they will wish to see horses whose training is proceeding along the right lines, and they will apply this perspective to their criteria. It is very important for the competitor to realise this; although it is highly desirable to try hard in a dressage test, the rider's efforts must be realistically based. He should avoid the error of taking a partly-trained horse into the arena and attempting to wring a Grand Prix level performance form him, since this will merely prove detrimental to the assets the horse currently possesses – he should, instead, try to do the basics well. To this end, he must be careful to avoid indulging any obsessions or pet theories as to what represents, or will produce 'good dressage'. This warning is not intended to be disparaging or condescending, but rather to draw attention to the fact that riding can become a very introspective and complex pursuit, and most riders would admit to confused phases when they could not see the wood for the trees, to the detriment of their performance.

Let us consider the judge's likely attitude towards key factors of the test, and the implications for the rider.

Impulsion

The judge will not, at this level, be expecting the tremendous impulsion necessary for correct performance of high school movements, but he will be thinking in terms of 'active forward movement' and 'energy under control'. He will place great emphasis upon the presence of such characteristics because, in common with all experienced horsemen, he will know that if a horse is not going freely forward, he will do nothing worthwhile.

The presence of impulsion does not, of course, *guarantee* a good performance, but its absence guarantees an indifferent one at best. Even if the rider can, to some extent, get away with it in a basic level test, inactivity is not indicative of correct training, and the test will be marked down on this basis. Errors of principle which produce inactive tests must, therefore, be avoided. Common errors are:

1) Attempting to quieten down a rather 'gassy' horse by sitting in a mouse-like way and asking nothing of him (i.e. under-riding). Although this may work at a superficial level it will, by definition, be at the expense of having the horse on the aids and working correctly. Furthermore, if the ploy fails in mid-test the rider may experience a sudden 'boiling-over' of the horse, and the latter part of the test may be reduced to a wrestling match as he seeks to apply hastily, makeshift controls.

2) Similarly, under-riding, born of the rider attempting to gain more thinking time in the arena, or of misconceptions that he is exhibiting collection or control, will (assuming that the horse in these examples is not a 'gassy' type) merely achieve a lifeless test, with the quality of gaits and transitions in particular in constant jeopardy.

3) Not asking enough of the horse. This may apply especially to hired horses. Many school horses are 'old soldiers' who may be quite capable, but are also quite happy to do as little work as possible. With such horses, the rider will certainly get only what he asks for. Of course, the time for assessment is when riding-in, and the rider must be prepared to be demanding of

this type of horse, and not just adopt the common attitude 'he doesn't do much, but at least he can walk, trot and canter.'
On the other hand, it is important that the rider does not confuse impulsion with speed, and either bustle the horse through the test as fast as his legs will carry him, or allow him to run around out of control.

Accuracy

It can be argued that total accuracy can only occur if all the characteristics of correct training are present to an advanced degree. This cannot be denied and, at advanced levels, accuracy will be assessed very much in this light.

However, at the levels under discussion, the judge is likely to consider accuracy less in terms of absolutes, and more as indicative of the horse's general standard of responses to the basic aids. This means that, while he will take a relatively lenient view of minor inaccuracies (although they will still be noted), more blatant inaccuracies will be marked down severely, the view being that, if a horse's training is to progress, he must learn to respond to the basic aids from an early stage.

The rider must, therefore, understand that inaccuracy will always be construed either as demonstrative of the horse's lack of training/response, or of error on his own part – in short, he will not get away with it, and he must concentrate upon riding all parts of the test as accurately as possible. Concentration is, in fact, the key word here; all tests are fairly concentrated, both in format and by the confines of the arena, and the rider who wishes for a good performance must remain alert and demanding of *himself*. Blaming the horse for inaccuracies which he should have foreseen and may have prevented is not going to persuade the judge to adjust this marks!

Outline

It is probably true to say that judges do not consider the horse's outline as a first priority. It is, however, an obvious indicator of the way in which the horse is moving, and the judge's attention is often drawn to the effects upon a horse's performance which result from a rider becoming preoccupied with this issue. This problem often affects those who are especially keen to do well.

Observing the highly-rounded topline of horses performing collected work at advanced level, people frequently develop the notion that is a *pre-requisite* of the dressage horse whereas, in fact, it is a *product* of progressive training. Although a fully trained horse will reach the stage at which he can substantially retain his outline in the required gaits and their variants, a partially trained horse will need to adapt his outline according to the demands made upon him. For example, his outline will appear longer and flatter when he is performing lengthened strides than when performing at a 'working' gait. If the rider makes the mistake of attempting to impose upon the horse a shape which, at his current stage of training, he cannot maintain without stresses and strains, this will prove markedly detrimental to his perform-ance. Common results include loss of free forward movement (with all that this entails), trailing hind limbs, tightness through the back, crookedness, and various evasions and resistances in the head and neck – usually the primary recipient area of the rider's misconceived ministrations.

Such errors will obviously have a serious effect upon the overall quality of the test and, consequently, upon the marks – including the collective marks awarded to the rider, who may feel mortified that his good intentions have been slighted. The fact is, however, that while judges will be obliged to look favourably upon a horse whose training is such that he can move *correctly* in a significantly rounded outline they will, at this level, be quite satisfied by what is often termed 'an improved natural outline' – i.e. that shown by a novice horse who is learning to accept the aids and carry himself and the rider in balance.

In order that the pitfalls mentioned may be avoided, let us clarify the influences upon the horse's outline. They are:
1) Skeletal structure.
2) Condition of musculature (poorly-muscled/slack/tight/well-muscled/supple).
3) Major source of propulsion (fore or hind limbs).
4) Acceptance of/responsiveness to aids.

To move correctly in a rounded outline, a horse must have at least reasonable skeletal structure, be well-muscled and supple, use the hind limbs as the main source of propulsion, and move readily forward from the rider's legs into his hands, flexing his poll and lower jaw. With the exception of skeletal structure, these factors relate directly to correct training, and will be principle concerns of the rider. The horse's overall carriage and outline will improve in strict relationship to his development in these areas, and will be impaired by deficiencies in any one of them. Attempts to ignore, avoid or short-circuit this state of affairs will inevitably create problems.

Other Criteria

The other criteria which judges are likely to apply are, in the main, listed in the 'collective marks' sections at the foot of the test sheets. These vary somewhat from test to test but, in total, they include all the characteristics of correct training, and various terms which describe aspects or indications of these characteristics (e.g. 'attention', 'confidence', 'calmness' as indications of acceptance of the aids). Since these terms apply to training in general, the judge will not consider them only in relation to the collective marks, but also, where applicable, throughout the test. The fact that a certain term is not itemised under the collective marks for a particular test does not mean that the judge will not consider it when assessing movements in the body of the test.

9

Riding-in

As far as the horse's performance is concerned, there are three main phases to the preparation for, and execution of, a dressage test. These are:

1) The whole background of training, the purpose of which is to improve the horse progressively in all departments.
2) The riding-in period immediately prior to the test, the object of which is to have the horse performing to the *best of his current ability* when he enters the arena.
3) The test itself, which is a *demonstration* of the horse's standard of training.

It is important to emphasise that the major processes of training belong to the first phase; the practise ground and test arena are not training venues (except insofar as a novice horse is introduced to a competition environment), they are, respectively, places for confirmation and presentation of the horse's training. Certainly, *all* riding has some influence upon training, but the rider who *starts* trying to teach his horse something new just before, or during, a test is to be more envied for his optimism than applauded for his practicality.

We shall consider the processes of riding-in in detail shortly but, before so doing, it is necessary to acknowledge the different circumstances which surround owner-riders and those who compete on hired horses. Owners, or those who ride a horse as a regular partnership, are likely to have made a significant contribution to the horse's prior training, and will thus be familiar with his general strengths, weaknesses and overall level of ability. The hirer, however, may have no such advantages; indeed, he may well be riding a horse he has never seen until the day of the test. Thus, whereas the owner-rider starts riding-in with considerable knowledge of his horse's capabilities, the hirer may have to assess them – perhaps very quickly – before he has a reasonable basis upon which to build a relevant riding-in programme.

Thus while the principles of riding-in apply to all riders, the practicalities vary markedly, and we shall therefore examine the process firstly as applicable to a regular partnership, and then give consideration to those circumstances of special relevance to the hirer. Riders in each category should give attention to both procedures; the hirer should consider that of the regular partnership because it represents the ideal, and the regular partner should consider that of the hirer on the following grounds:

1) He may, someday, be in the same position.
2) In order to achieve a degree of success, the hiring rider must become especially analytical in his thinking and effective in his riding; qualities which can only enhance the ability of any rider.
3) It may help him appreciate his own good fortune.

The Regular Partnership

MENTAL APPROACH Because the riding-in period is so important, the rider's mental attitude and approach to it are crucial. If he is in the wrong frame of mind, or thinking along the wrong lines, the quality of work performed is almost certain to suffer.

The potential for some of the main problems which may confront the regular partner lies rooted in his very familiarity with the horse. Great advantage though this is, the danger exists that the rider may develop a tendency to make assumptions – for better or worse – about how the horse is *going* to perform, on the basis of what he has done in the past. At first sight, this may not seem unreasonable, and it is certain that the rider can neither alter the past, nor expunge it from his memory. Even if he could do so, the latter action would be entirely undesirable, since it would undermine the basis of the learning processes. However, there is a world of difference between drawing upon past experience for indications of how the horse is *likely* to respond in various circumstances, and making concrete pre-judgements or fatalistic assumptions. The former entails the relevant use of acquired knowledge, while the latter is based on the premise that the horse is bound to do what he has done in the past – the logical extension of which is that all attempts at training are a waste of time. Put this way, it may seem insulting even to suggest that an intelligent rider might fall into this way of thinking, but the practise arena can easily become a place of emotion rather than logic. The mental attitudes to guard against are:

1) Assuming that the horse is bound to perform a certain movement poorly, and either:

   a. Avoiding it altogether whilst riding-in, hoping for the best in the test itself. The philosophy may be that the rider does not want to upset the horse or jolt his own confidence, but the logic is the same as an actor not rehearsing certain lines because they contain words he finds hard to pronounce!

   b. Practising the movement with a defeatist attitude, so that the rider does not ride to the best of his own ability, thereby making his assumption come true.

   c. Approaching the movement with a clenched-teeth determination to wring a sudden improvement from the horse. Although determination is an essential quality in the rider, it must be coupled with a coherent strategy, and the likely result of 'going at it bald-headed' is that the horse will become as tense as the rider and perform even worse than anticipated. This can create the starting point for a downward spiral in the relationship between horse and rider, which may spread beyond the original area of concern.

2) Assuming that the horse is bound to perform a certain movement well, and thus becoming blasé, and not riding the movement to the best of the rider's ability. The horse will inevitably respond by not performing as well as expected, thereby inducing disappointment, annoyance or mild panic in the rider, none of which is conducive to good riding.

   In order to avoid such attitudes, the rider should approach the riding-in period with as open a mind as possible, and a determination to ride the horse as he is at present, and not as he may be remembered from the previous day, week or test. He must also be prepared to ride very thoughtfully, self-critically and – at all times – to the best of his ability, bearing in mind the need to build mutual confidence as well as attending to the technical side.

RIDER'S AIMS   In addition to the fundamental necessity to have the horse moving actively forward, the rider's main aims are to promote/enhance suppleness and attentiveness and, ideally, to induce in the horse a heightened desire to perform. Before discussing these aims in the context of the riding-in period, it may be helpful to look at them individually.

Suppleness: For our purposes, we shall define suppleness as optimium elasticity of the muscles and flexibility of the joints. These are essential pre-requisites for peak performance in any athlete – human or equine – and it will be noted that all serious sportsmen, gymnasts, dancers etc. concentrate the early stages of their practise seasons almost exclusively upon limbering up. As far as the horse is concerned, the degree of suppleness achieved will have a direct influence upon the quality of all the characteristics of correct training. It is, therefore, counter-productive to start actually *working* a horse who is cold, 'tight' or tense, and the first part of a riding-in session should be given over mainly to promoting suppleness.

Attentiveness: Attentiveness may be considered as consisting of two phases; the horse's concentration/willingness to 'listen' to the rider, and his actual responses to the aids. For reasons already stated, the latter will be of higher quality in the supple horse; thus, within reason, the rider should concentrate less on attentiveness than on suppleness in the opening minutes of the riding-in period. In some instances, however, it can be necessary to give the matter consideration *before* starting the riding-in session proper. This condition applies particularly in the case of young, inexperienced horses or those who (for whatever reason) become unduly excited/distracted by a competition – or otherwise unfamiliar – environment.

If the rider suspects that his horse fits into one of these categories, he should allow an extra half-hour or so before the time he has allotted for riding-in, and should walk the horse quietly around the competition ground, letting him have a good look at unfamiliar sights. Special attention should be paid (if possible) to anything potentially alarming in the vicinity of the test arena (this may include marker boards, flowers etc. as well as flapping tents and tannoy systems) although, of course, the horse must not be taken into the arena, or ridden near it while another competitor is in action. Any nervousness on the horse's part should be met with reassurance, but any tendency to nap towards stable companions or horse box must be firmly curbed.

Gradually, the rider can ask the horse to pay less attention to his surroundings and more to himself, and, once a more responsive attitude becomes apparent, the riding-in session can commence.

Heightened desire to perform: Improving the horse's suppleness and attentiveness will certainly enhance his *capacity* to perform, but this is not necessarily the same as enhancing his *desire* to do so. Although the psychology of the horse is something of a grey area, there is no doubt that – in the right circumstances – horses exhibit signs which we can only construe as indicative of pleasure, enjoyment, eagerness and enthusiasm. These are often remarked upon in the context of equestrian sport 'he *loves* his hunting/to jump/to race', etc. and indicate (hopefully) that the horse's mental attitude is in fruitful harmony with that of his rider.

Since dressage is fundamentally concerned with training (i.e. work), it is possible that it may not have the immediate appeal to the horse of pursuits which he would find inherently more exciting. Nevertheless, it remains an important ideal for the rider that the horse should enjoy this work. This is not merely altruism; a *desire* (eagerness) to perform at dressage will be shown chiefly by the ready generation of impulsion and by ready co-operation – very real and valuable assets for the rider.

Of course, a horse cannot be *made* eager and enthusiastic; the rider can only do his best to promote conditions under which he might reasonably be expected to adopt such an attitude. The horse's long-term outlook in life will be a major influence in this respect, and the owner-rider should give constant and serious attention to the contributing factors. However, the short-term influence, which is our main concern at present, is the rider's attitude to the horse during the riding-in period. The rider must remain mindful that, while he is seeking to elicit the highest level of performance from the horse, this entails the horse being confident and willing. He must therefore be careful that, with the stresses of competition upon himself, he does not put so much mental or physical pressure on the horse that these qualities, or the potential for them, become impaired. To give a few examples, the rider must remember not to work the horse incessantly, he must be sure to praise/reward good responses, and he must correct faults, errors and disobediences quietly, calmly and logically, trying, if anything, to exercise more patience than he might do during training sessions at home.

RIDING-IN PROGRAMME It would be unrealistic to lay down a hard and fast schedule for riding-in, or to suggest that such would be ideal for every horse. However, having a general scheme around which to work will prove much more productive than attempting to proceed in a disorganised, random manner.

The first thing the rider must do is allow himself sufficient time to ride-in thoroughly and unhurriedly. The optimum time for riding-in is likely to vary a little from horse to horse – perhaps even from test to test – but it is important that a timescale is set, and it is sensible to err on the side of generosity. There is no satisfactory remedy for having too little time, and hurried, truncated riding-in sessions will have serious repercussions in the test arena. On the other hand, having more time than proves necessary need not be a drawback at all – provided it is used sensibly. Thus the rider who finds he has spare time should not indulge in aimless repetitions, but should simply adjust the workload by spending more time at walk (although this must be correct walk, performed to some purpose). If there is no risk of the horse getting cold, it may also be appropriate to pause at suitable intervals, which will both give the horse a breather and allow the rider to marshal his thoughts.

By way of a general indication, it is unlikely that horses performing at the levels under discussion would need, or benefit from, riding-in for more than an hour, but to allocate less than forty-five minutes would be inadvisable. The riding-in period should be gauged to finish just a few minutes before the scheduled test time, and it must not be impinged upon. Therefore, the rider should ensure that sufficient *extra* time is allowed for unboxing, tacking-up, declaring entries, finding the loo, and the other paraphenalia associated with participating in an equestrian event.

Once at the riding-in area, it is important to assess the realities of the environment. In some cases, it may be possible to influence them (for instance, if there are a lot of flies about, repellent should be applied *before* trying to achieve a steady head carriage) but, in general, it will be necessary to adapt. This entails being mindful of matters such as avoiding collisions with fellow competitors in a restricted area, not working more than necessary at the faster gaits in hot weather, expecting some reaction from a horse asked to move directly into driving rain, and making some allowance for bad ground conditions.

Although it is an unusual situation, special consideration should be given to circumstances where the main riding-in area is indoors, and the test is to be performed outside in adverse conditions. If the riding-in takes place entirely indoors, the sudden change of environment may adversely affect the horse's performance at a critical moment. Thus it is best, where possible, to spend the last part of the session outside, to give him time to acclimatise. This means, of course, that he may initially not go as well as he has been, but the rider should bear in mind the purpose of his ploy, and not panic.

Once such matters have been taken into account, riding-in can commence. The following is a suggested outline.

Phase one: Main emphasis upon warming-up; initial suppleness. Five minutes free walk on a long rein. Rider should not be over-demanding, expecting just a reasonable degree of activity. In the event of actual sluggishness, this should not be countered with nagging or 'bustling' leg aids, but by prompt and correct use of the schooling whip. Horse should not be ridden repeatedly around arena perimeter, but in a series of simple figures based on 20 metre circles and turns across the arena.

Five minutes working trot. Rider rising and maintaining a light contact, riding horse in a relatively long 'frame' and occasionally offering him the opportunity to stretch his head and neck right down. (It is at this juncture that horses with a tendency to stuffiness of the upper respiratory tract will often snort, blow and clear themselves out – actions which will render them more amenable to flexing and working on the bit in due course.) Simple figures on both reins, as in walk.

Short period of walk on a long rein. Medium walk, beginning to ask the horse for more response. Through working trot to a brief canter, e.g. once round the arena, incorporating a 20 metre circle, on each rein. Two or three minutes walk on a long rein, during which time the rider can assess how the horse is warming up by noting freedom and activity of movement.

Phase two: Working to achieve optimum levels of activity, suppleness and attentiveness, thereby promoting the characteristics of correct training.

Early work at medium walk, later work mainly at trot, with occasional periods of walk. At walk, figures based upon medium sized (10–12 metre) circles, with emphasis on correct bend, and encouraging flexion of poll and lower jaw by 'offering' a soft contact with the inside rein. Figure work interspersed with work in straight lines.

At trot, similar figures, plus leg-yielding and shoulder-in (if the horse is capable). Transitions between halt-walk-trot and half-halts, with emphasis on aids and transitions flowing from the hindquarters forward. If required in the test, lengthened strides, with attention to smooth changes from and to working gait.

If the horse tends to be excitable, there should be increased emphasis on circle-based work. If he tends to be phlegmatic or lazy, there should be more emphasis on vigorous straight line work.

Short period at walk, noting horse's reaction when offered long rein. Work at medium walk, practising square halts, rein-back if applicable. Through trot to canter, seeking good transitions up and down, horse working in an improved outline compared to first canter, circles and figures as appropriate to test. Period at walk, gradually allowing horse to 'take' rein.

Phase three: Practising such movements as rider thinks beneficial. Any problematical movements to be approached with great discretion, and certainly not at the last moment. The session should finish with the performance of whatever simple relevant work the rider can – as nearly as possible – guarantee that the partnership will do well.

During the riding-in session, it is most helpful if there is someone on hand to ascertain whether the competition is running to time, or, if it is running late, by how much. The rider will then be in a position to pad out the later stages with more walk, so that he does not complete his programme only to find that he will not be in the test arena for another half hour.

The Rider and Hired Horse Partnership

MENTAL APPROACH Riding a good dressage test on an unfamiliar horse is no easy task, and the riding-in period will, necessarily, be very demanding of the rider. However, while there is no point in pretending that this is not the case, it is most important not to start out with the feeling that the task is overwhelming or impossible. Firstly, providing the exercise is undertaken whole-heartedly, the worst that can happen is that the rider will gain valuable experience from riding another horse. Secondly, assuming that the horse is hired from some sort of commercial establishment, it is wrong to imagine that he will necessarily be ill-suited to the task. Certainly, the quality and ability of riding-school horses varies tremendously, but those supplied by a decent establishment should be quite capable of performing a reasonable basic-level test; the majority of the test requirements being familiar movements and figures of the riding school. Indeed, in club level competitions, school horses have often shown themselves capable of doing as well as – if not better than – those in private ownership.

RIDER'S AIMS The aims of riding-in are the same for hirer as for owner, but with the additional need to assess and become familiar with the horse. Ideally, therefore, the hirer should allow more time for riding-in than might be necessary for a regular partnership but, in practice, this may not be possible. Indeed, at some minor, less formal competitions, there may be only a few minutes available.

Preliminary information: The hirer cannot afford to waste time, and must make maximum use of every available moment – though not at the expense of becoming flustered, and hurrying the horse. He can help his cause by beginning to assess the horse from first sight, but it is important that, in his desire for rapid information, he does not fall into the assumption trap already mentioned. Until he actually rides the horse, he will be dealing with opinions and impressions; these may prove perfectly correct, but they must be substantiated before their value is confirmed. In this respect, the rider should be especially wary of verbal information given about a horse. This is often offered freely but, unless it comes from an experienced and trusted source it is best taken with a large pinch of salt. For various reasons, opinions offered by stable staff often prove so unreliable that one wonders whether they are discussing the right animal, and opinions of other riders may be prejudiced or ill-founded.

Reverting to the evidence of his own eyes, the rider should first assess the horse's conformation to the best of his ability. This can give fairly solid clues about how the horse is likely to move, and may provide reasons for difficulties encountered in riding, which the rider can take into account when trying overcome them. Some straightforward examples are:

1) A horse with heavy shoulders and little development of the quarters is likely to move on the forehand.
2) Significant muscular development beneath the neck at the

expense of muscle along the crest is indicative that the horse moves in a hollow outline.

3) A big, long-backed horse is likely to find it relatively difficult to maintain balance and bend in the confines of the arena.

These examples have in common the fact that they represent drawbacks which have, at best, long-term solutions through remedial training. In the context of a 'one off' ride, where the purpose is to get the best from the horse as he is at present, the rider should think in terms of making the best of things as they exist. It would, for instance, be totally counter-productive to get irritated with the horse in the last example on the grounds that he is 'just a clumsy brute'.

In a similar vein, it is possible to form a preliminary opinion of the horse's temperament by noting various characteristics as they appear, and gearing initial aid applications accordingly. Care must be taken, however, to avoid an extreme starting point; the highly-strung, fidgety horse will probably benefit from quiet, calm handling, but he will certainly not benefit from total lack of direction from the saddle. On the other hand, the horse who *appears* sluggish must be given a chance to respond to normal aid applications before the rider resorts to stronger measures.

An additional opportunity for gaining information will occur if the horse is first ridden by another competitor. In this case, observation is natural and useful, and much of value may be gleaned but, again, caution is the order of the day. It must be borne in mind that few horses go exactly the same for different riders (even riders of similar experience and ability), and that the horse may naturally perform better or worse second time round. Also, although the more experienced competitor may note problems and their apparent solutions when observing another rider, he is not certain to be aware of all the contributing factors or their precise effects. The possible permutations in this respect are endless, but to give a simple (and by no means absurd) example, it could be that the struggling, uncomfortable fellow competitor is having more difficulty with an unsatisfactory saddle than with the horse.

Assessment from the saddle: Having gained as much preliminary information about the horse as is possible, the rider can address himself to the practicalities of riding-in. His task of assessing and becoming familiar with the horse must continue in tandem with work on suppleness and attentiveness, but there are certain moments when assessment should be given special attention. These are:

Firstly, in the opening minutes, when the rider should assess the horse's initial responses at a time when he is not being particularly demanding, and is applying the aids in the light of his own first impressions. The chief purpose at this juncture is to answer his own inevitable question 'what sort of feel does this horse give me now that I'm on his back?'

Secondly, in the few minutes after he starts to be more demanding of the horse – the first, and major, demand being for an acceptable degree of active forward movement. We have already discussed how the existence of this quality of forward movement will have positive effects upon the other characteristics of training regardless of the state of their development, and it is therefore essential that it is established before the rider makes firm judgements of his horse's capabilities. This is because, once the horse is moving actively forwards, apparent problems may diminish, and the rider will be able to assess more accurately the root cause of those which remain, and tailor his riding accordingly. For example, an inactive horse may move hollow-backed, or with incorrect lateral bend either because he is resisting/evading the rider, or mainly because of congenital defects or established training faults. If, once he is moving actively forwards, these problems greatly diminish, the rider can be pretty certain the former was the case, and that he has found the cure. If, however, they diminish but little, then it is likely that the problems are deep-seated, and, in his present situation, the rider will have to work with, or around, them.

Thirdly, in the light of such aid modifications as he feels are appropriate. The rider of an unfamiliar horse should be prepared to modify his aids as and when he feels this may prove fruitful. His objective is to find the most effective way to communicate with the horse, and this may involve communicating in terms with which the horse is familiar and/or which take account of any particular difficulties, even if they are not in strict accord with the rider's conception of what is correct. This is not to say that the rider ought to experiment with bizarre or illogical aids, but simply that he may benefit by remaining flexible in his approach. To give a simple example, one horse might only respond to canter aids which involved a definite lightening of the rein contact, and strong use of the legs, while another might respond to the lightest of leg pressure, and no discernible alteration in rein contact. The latter might reasonably be considered a much better-schooled horse but, regardless of which aids are correct or incorrect, both are, in our context, effective on the horse in question, and both would be inappropriate if applied on the other.

Heightened desire to perform: It is true that this characteristic may not be produced as readily in a horse whose daily routine includes two or three hours in the school as it is in a privately-owned horse. Nevertheless, the principles still apply, and it is worth noting that the horse whose general attitude to school work is one of indifference may perk up noticeably when ridden by someone who both insists that he moves actively forward and allows him to do so.

RIDING-IN PROGRAMME Given time, the programme for the hirer should be similar to that outlined for the regular partner, with modifications as appropriate for their particular horse. This suggestion, however, would be of little practical value to a competitor who has only fifteen minutes to ride-in. On the other hand, attempting to detail a shortened programme might tempt the rider with more time available to imagine that such a programme was considered sufficient, when it would only be intended as a suggestion of how to make the best of difficult circumstances. The best advice, therefore, may simply be to make maximum use of whatever time is available, and to follow the general progression of the programme already outlined. This can be briefly summarised thus:

Warming up, with initial assessment of how horse 'feels'. Work to promote suppleness and attentiveness – special emphasis on activity, rhythm, straightness, accuracy. Finding out how best to cope with inherent difficulties.

Work on parts of the test – finding out how horse responds to any special requirements (rein-back, lengthened strides etc.) and making mental note to modify ambitions in test if horse appears unfamiliar with any particular demands.

Finish with anything simple and relevant which will boost mutual confidence of horse and rider.

10

Riding the Test

Riding the test should be seen as the culmination of a period of preparation and attention to the principles of dressage. It is mainly a product of what has gone before, in the same way as the first night of a play is the product of weeks of planning and rehearsal. There is no reason to suppose that a horse's performance in the test will be any better than his recent work outside, and the only reasons why it might be any worse are: bad conditions, external distractions and the rider's mental attitude. The first two factors may well be totally beyond the rider's control (although how he copes with them will depend upon experience and approach), but his own mental attitude is of major importance.

Destructive attitudes divide basically into over-confidence on the one hand, and lack of confidence/nervousness on the other. The former, though rare, has been observed, but usually teaches its own salutary lessons. The latter, in various forms and degrees, is common, and it may assist afflicted riders if they consider the following. Instead of thinking in terms of 'getting it over with', the rider should think of presenting the test. This evokes the idea of *showing* what the horse can do, rather than apologising for it. It also sums up what the rider who enters a test is doing, that is saying 'this is a demonstration of my riding and the horse's training – please comment'.

Pursuing a similar train of thought, it should be remembered that judges, like doctors, have 'seen it all before'. This is especially true of those who normally judge the more basic levels of dressage, many of whom are professional instructors who daily have to adopt an understanding and sympathetic approach to riders' problems. This does not, of course, mean that they will give a test a better mark than it deserves, but it should mean that any criticism will be constructive.

It is important that a positive approach is maintained during the test itself, especially in moments of difficulty. It should be remembered that the test is marked basically as a series of individual movements, and, if things go wrong at some stage the golden rules is don't panic, but re-establish an equilibrium as calmly and promptly as possible. In this way, the damage can be confined, hopefully, to a single movement and, at worst, to a small segment of the test. If, however, the rider panics or gives up mentally, a moment's error can have repercussions throughout the remainder of the test.

The philosophy of staying calm applies equally to errors of course. Although a single error carries only a two mark penalty, many riders view the possibility with a disproportionate degree of dread and assume that, in the event of an error, they will become hopelessly distracted. In fact, providing the test has been learnt thoroughly, an error is likely to be the result of a moment's aberration; as soon as the stop signal is heard, realisation will dawn, and the correct route spring to mind. However, it is not in the rider's interest to resume too hurriedly; a brief moment to marshal the thoughts and prepare the horse can prove beneficial. If the rider really has got lost, it is best to confess to the judge, who will doubtless provide a thorough prompt. This course of action is, at least, less embarrassing than muddling on regardless, risking further errors and perhaps riding badly due to preoccupation with route.

If, then, the rider has prepared properly, and is in a positive frame of mind, performing the test is just a matter of going into the arena and riding as well as possible. Although there is much talk of 'ringcraft', this is really just a manifestation of the well-prepared rider's clarity of thought and effectiveness.

11

Learning from the Judge's Remarks

We should perhaps begin this topic by acknowledging that dressage judges, like other groups of people, vary markedly in their competence, perception and opinions. However, the purpose here is not to offer criticisms of judges or judging standards, but to explain how the rider may benefit by paying attention to the judge's comment.s To this end, it should be borne in mind that any judge should be, at least, an experienced, unbiased observer, whose opinions are worthy of serious consideration.

Everyone naturally wants to do well, and it is very easy for a competitor to feel slighted, or adopt a negative attitude, if he considers that the judge has been harsh. A common reaction (especially amongst riders of hired horses) is along the lines of 'the judge should try riding it'. Although this might sometimes prove illuminating, it misses the point; the judge's brief is not to ride horses, but to assess how they perform when ridden by the competitors. Furthermore, since he is assessing standards of training, a judge can hardly be expected to show leniency to a horse who is difficult, however much he may sympathise with the rider.

As far as the actual level of marks is concerned, this must also be seen in perspective. It is true that unsatisfactory and complicated repercussions may arise if a judge fails to make reasonable allowance for the general standard of competition, but it is also true that no-one's real interests are served if a judge is too lenient. Therefore, the inexperienced competitor in particular must come to terms with the fact that mere performance of a movement does not entitle him to a good mark; if he wants good marks, the movements must be performed *well*. In this respect, he may learn much by comparing his own evaluations with those of the judge, and his marks in general with those of a fellow competitor he acknowledges as being of a higher standard than his own.

The judge's marks, and comments, fall into two categories; those awarded for each movement, and the collective marks awarded at the end of the test. The full scale of marks and their official interpretations are:

10 excellent	6 satisfactory	2 bad
9 very good	5 sufficient	1 very bad
8 good	4 insufficient	0 not executed
7 fairly good	3 fairly bad	

The further definition of 'not executed' is 'that nothing which is required has been performed'. Coupled with error of course rules, this means, at basic levels, there can be only very rare circumstances in which 0 can be correctly awarded.

The judge's remarks made during individual movements must necessarily be brief, and the official interpretations supplement them and, in some cases, suffice without embellishment. For example, if a mark of 8 is given, a comment 'good' is strictly unnecessary – though it will often appear because judges naturally tend to think out loud before awarding a mark. In other circumstances, however, the remarks column assumes greater significance. When a movement consists of more than one identifiable element, it is possible that the elements may be performed to different standards. In such a case, the mark given for the movement must be a compromise, which the judge will wish to clarify. If, for example, a movement consists of a circle at canter followed by a transition to trot, the judge might observe 'good canter circle, slightly late to trot.' Had the standard attained in the canter circle been maintained, the judge would have been obliged (deeming it 'good') to award 8. However, in the light of the late transition, he will adjust the mark to – probably – 7.

In cases where a low mark is given, a reasonable judge will usually feel it appropriate to say why this is so. While no-one likes to receive a poor mark, an accurate summary in such circumstances can prove informative and instructive – for instance, a remark such as '4 – ran onto forehand in canter transition' may actually *help* the rider more than a bland '6 – satisfactorily'.

The collective marks provide an opportunity for the judge to comment in more depth on his overall impressions. Since the criteria listed in the collective sections will have had integral influences upon the movements of the test, there should be a strong corellation between the average marks awarded for the movements, and the average of the collective marks. However, the collective section allows the judge to highlight strengths and weaknesses in the horse's overall training/performance. For example, the average mark given per movement might be 6, but the judge may consider that the horse shows an imbalance between impulsion and calmness, so he might award 7 for the one, and 5 for the other.

It is when making remarks in connection with the collective marks that the judge has most time (and space) available, and he may offer comments which prove very helpful. These, therefore, are worthy of special consideration, and should not be lightly dismissed while the competitor is in a state of post-test collapse, or still taking umbrage at only getting 4 for rein-back! It is, in fact, worthwhile keeping old test sheets, and it is surprising how often, looking back in the light of experience, one will acknowledge that a judge was justified in making a certain remark, or, alternatively, gain a reminder of how to deal with a continuing problem.

Conclusion

Much of the challenge and fascination of dressage lies in the fact that it is not a sport of absolutes; even a mark of 10 denotes excellence rather than perfection. Thus success must always be considered in relative terms, being not so much a matter of attaining final goals as of maintaining progress.

It is important to realise that there is nothing mystical about this process; the chief criteria are attention to detail and a continuing desire to improve communications with the horse. The former is unquestionably within the compass of any rider of average intelligence. As far as the latter is concerned, it is true that some people have more natural rapport and empathy with horses than others. However, it should be borne in mind that, compared to a human being, a horse is a simple creature, and it is on *his* terms that we must communicate. Thus there are two points of which the rider seeking better communication must be constantly aware: firstly, although riding effectively cannot be described as easy, it can never, by definition, be complicated. Secondly, while the rider's aim is unquestionably to become the senior partner, the horse/rider partnership will only flourish where the rider is prepared for the communication to be two-way.